AFTER GOD'S

OWN

HEART

With much hope and
with thanks for
your work in the
past.

[signature]

23 . x . 2017

THE GOSPEL ACCORDING TO THE OLD TESTAMENT

A series of studies on the lives
of Old Testament characters, written for
laypeople and pastors, and designed to
encourage Christ-centered reading, teaching,
and preaching of the Old Testament

TREMPER LONGMAN III
J. ALAN GROVES

Series Editors

AFTER GOD'S OWN HEART

HEART

THE GOSPEL ACCORDING TO
DAVID

MARK J. BODA

P&R
PUBLISHING
P.O. BOX 817 • PHILLIPSBURG • NEW JERSEY 08865-0817

Page design by Tobias Design

Printed in the United States of America

Library of Congress Cataloging-in-Publication Data

Boda, Mark J.
    After God's own heart : the Gospel according to David / Mark J. Boda.
        p. cm. —   (The Gospel according to the Old Testament)
    Includes bibliographical references and index.
    ISBN-13: 978-0-87552-653-9 (pbk.)
  1.   David, King of Israel—Textbooks. 2.   Typology (Theology)—Textbooks.
3.   Messiah—Prophecies—Textbooks. 4.   Bible. O.T.—Relation to the New Testament—Textbooks. 5.   Bible. N.T.—Relation to the Old Testament—Textbooks.   I. Title.
    BS580.D3B57 2007
    222'.4092—dc22
                                                                                        2007017176

ad majorem Dei gloriam

Dedicated to David Christian on the occasion of his twentieth birthday

CONTENTS

FOREWORD

The New Testament is in the Old concealed;
the Old Testament is in the New revealed.
—Augustine

Concerning this salvation, the prophets, who spoke of the grace that was to come to you, searched intently and with the greatest care, trying to find out the time and circumstances to which the Spirit of Christ in them was pointing when he predicted the sufferings of Christ and the glories that would follow. It was revealed to them that they were not serving themselves but you, when they spoke of the things that have now been told you by those who have preached the gospel to you by the Holy Spirit sent from heaven. Even angels long to look into these things. (1 Peter 1:10–12)

"In addition, some of our women amazed us. They went to the tomb early this morning but didn't find his body. They came and told us that they had seen a vision of angels, who said he was alive. Then some of our companions went to the tomb and found it just as the women had said, but him they did not see."

He said to them, "How foolish you are, and how slow of heart to believe all that the prophets have spoken! Did not the Christ have to suffer these things and then enter his glory?" And beginning with Moses and all the Prophets, he explained to them what was said in all the Scriptures concerning himself. (Luke 24:22–27)

The prophets searched. Angels longed to see. And the disciples didn't understand. But Moses, the prophets, and all the Old Testament Scriptures had spoken about it—that Jesus would come, suffer, and then be glorified. God began to tell a story in the Old Testament, the ending of which the audience eagerly anticipated. But the Old Testament audience was left hanging. The plot was laid out but the climax was delayed. The unfinished story begged an ending. In Christ, God has provided the climax to the Old Testament story. Jesus did not arrive unannounced; his coming was declared *in advance* in the Old Testament, not just in explicit prophecies of the Messiah but by means of the stories of all of the events, characters, and circumstances in the Old Testament. God was telling a larger, overarching, unified story. From the account of creation in Genesis to the final stories of the return from exile, God progressively unfolded his plan of salvation. And the Old Testament account of that plan always pointed in some way to Christ.

AIMS OF THIS SERIES

The Gospel According to the Old Testament Series is committed to the proposition that the Bible, both Old and New Testaments, is a unified revelation of God, and that its thematic unity is found in Christ. The individual books of the Old Testament exhibit diverse genres, styles, and individual theologies, but tying them all together is the constant foreshadowing of, and pointing forward to, Christ. Believing in the fundamentally Christocentric nature of the Old Testament, as well as the New Testament, we offer this series of studies in the Old Testament with the following aims:

- to lay out the pervasiveness of the revelation of Christ in the Old Testament
- to promote a Christ-centered reading of the Old Testament
- to encourage Christ-centered preaching and teaching from the Old Testament

To this end, the volumes in this series are written for pastors and laypeople, not scholars.

While such a series could take a number of different shapes, we have decided, in most cases, to focus individual volumes on Old Testament figures—people—rather than books or themes. Some books, of course, will receive major attention in connection with their authors or main characters (e.g., Daniel or Isaiah). Also, certain themes will be emphasized in connection with particular figures.

It is our hope and prayer that this series will revive interest in and study of the Old Testament as readers recognize that the Old Testament points forward to Jesus Christ.

TREMPER LONGMAN III
J. ALAN GROVES

TRIBUTE TO J. ALAN GROVES

After the death of Ray Dillard in 1993, Al Groves and I saw to the publication of our beloved friend, mentor, and colleague's book, *Faith in the Face of Apostasy*, and in doing so launched a new series. This series, the Gospel According the Old Testament, aims to show, as Christ himself declared, that "all the Scriptures" speak of our Lord's suffering and glorification (Luke 24:27). It is with sadness at our loss that I report that Al Groves recently died at the age of fifty-four. Our sadness is tempered by the joy we feel that he is now with the Lord he loved and served so well in this life. We owe Al for his insightful teaching, his incisive writing, his work on the Hebrew text for computer use, and, for those of us who knew him, his friendship and encouragement.

TREMPER LONGMAN III

PREFACE

It was surprisingly in a course on missiology that I first
fell in love with biblical theology. Harvie Conn told us
in the first class that he taught that particular course in
a cycle, one year addressing practical missiological issues,
the other biblical theological foundations for missions. He
must have done it to keep it interesting for himself because
no one ever could or did (though they probably should
have) take the course twice (that is, unless . . .). I had
grown up in a denomination with a rich heritage of missions, but what I heard that semester offered the richest
and deepest biblical foundation for missions that I ever had
encountered. Professor Conn took us on a panoramic journey over the mountaintops and into the valleys of the history of revelation in order to show us that God's passion
for the nations was the backbone of the redemptive story
from beginning to end.

One of my final encounters with biblical theology at
Westminster comes immediately to mind as well. It
occurred near the end of my time at the seminary. My
brother Matt was unable to take Ray Dillard's prophets
course in the final semester. He had discovered through
the underground Westminster rumor mill that one of our
fellow students, Pam to be precise, had taped the entire
semester of Dr. Dillard's riveting lectures (and they were
that indeed), and she was willing to lend them to Matt.
My brother, brave soul that he was, had an idea. He would
approach Ray's colleague, Bruce Waltke, and ask him if
he would be willing to supervise him in an independent

study on the prophets based on Ray Dillard's taped lectures. Well, not only was Dr. Waltke delighted to supervise my brother, but he also wanted to listen to the same tapes and then get together with Matt once a week or so (there is some discrepancy on whether this was to be once a week or less frequent) to discuss the content.

Faced with the prospect of meeting with his former intermediate Hebrew professor alone and knowing that I was heading toward a career in Old Testament and Hebrew studies, Matt thought it would be great if I would join the two of them for these regular "supervisions." We decided to kick the semester off with a bang. We invited Dr. Waltke out for breakfast at the local Bob's Big Boy to enjoy their all-you-can-eat buffet. We all arrived on time and piled our plates high with food. Sitting down to dig in, Dr. Waltke thought it would be nice if we began the session by each asking a question about the tapes we had heard. My brother Matt began (well, he got us into this situation!), and the question was something about the relationship between Samuel and Elijah as prophets. All I can remember is Dr. Waltke's eyes going up above his eyelids in classic fashion (as in that class when the power went out and he lectured for ten minutes in the darkness before realizing the lights were off) and, as if he was reading some notes off the inside of his eyelids, he began to review the history of prophetism from Moses to Jesus, via Samuel, Elijah, Elisha, Isaiah, Jeremiah, Ezekiel, and straight through to Zechariah, Malachi, and John the Baptist. There we sat, a bit terrified at the prospect of discussing such deep theological insight with the master and wondering if we were ever going to eat our pancakes and sausages which were quickly going cold. To be truthful, so overwhelmed were we (or at least one of us) that it was the one and only meeting of that semester. What I experienced that day, however, was the power of biblical theology to offer cohesion to the diverse literature and history found within the Bible. And what I observed that day was the passion of one who had spent a lifetime searching these Scriptures.

These two events stand as bookends on an education in biblical theology that could be discerned in every class (Longman, Dillard, Groves, Silva, McCartney, Poythress, Gaffin, Ferguson, Barker, Logan, Davis, Ortiz, Bettler, Sibley). One final course, however, cannot go without mention, and especially in light of the fact that this professor has recently entered the manifest presence of the Lord of redemptive history.

I had always wanted to take a course with Edmund Clowney, a professor who had taught my own father at Westminster in the early '60s, and my opportunity came in the January term in my middle year when Dr. Clowney came to teach an intensive course on Preaching Christ from the Old Testament. There I was shaped by one who challenged us to take into account the ultimate context of all biblical revelation, that is, the grand story of redemption that finds its culmination in the first and second coming of Jesus Christ. We were encouraged to end each sermon by showing the way in which the truth of the passage we were preaching pointed toward and was ultimately fulfilled in the gospel of Jesus Christ.

As the week wore on we were mesmerized by the ability of this man to always find a link to the gospel whether he was preaching in Leviticus or Obadiah, Ecclesiastes or Chronicles. Finally, one of the students asked the question that we all were dying to ask but felt too intimidated to venture. The student was concerned that there were many practical applications in the various Old Testament passages that he had consistently overlooked on his way to preaching Christ. In what way was such Christological preaching relevant to the lives of his people who were looking for guidance on everyday issues that many of these Old Testament passages addressed? Dr. Clowney's response was quick but gentle as he returned the question with some of his own, which in my paraphrases are: "What could be more relevant than the good news that Jesus Christ has died and rose again? What could be more practical than the new life that we experience in and through Jesus' sacrifice for us?" Well, what could one say in response to that? Dr. Clowney was right and reminded us that the ultimate context of every passage of Scripture is the grand story of redemption that must not be lost in Christian proclamation today.

I hope this short book will honor the rich biblical theological tradition that has set Westminster apart from its inception. Upon the shoulders of greats like Conn, Waltke, and Clowney, who in turn were standing upon other giants like Vos, Young, and Machen, I steady myself as I seek to interpret the ancient story of David in light of the gospel of Jesus Christ. For this privilege I am thankful to my former professors, Tremper Longman and Al Groves. Tremper's enduring friendship through the years and Al's patient endurance in the midst of suffering have extended their impact well beyond the classrooms where they first captured my imagination for the literature of the Old Testament.

While writing this book I have enjoyed the hospitality and friendship of my father-in-law and mother-in-law, David and Ruth Rambo. Not only do their names foreshadow key characters in the drama that this book will trace, but their lives embody the values that will challenge us to live as that descendant of David, Jesus Christ. In light of this, as well as their unconditional love and acceptance and their enduring encouragement and support of their son-in-law as a Christian academic throughout eight years of graduate work and now thirteen years of teaching, I want to express publicly my appreciation to them.

Providentially, I am completing the preface to this book as my eldest son's twentieth birthday approaches. His name, David Christian, not only sums up the core themes of this book but also my deepest hopes for his life. My prayer for you, David, is that the themes from Scripture to which this book point may become a reality in your life as you seek our Savior, the son of David, Jesus the Christ. May you be truly a "man after God's own heart" (1 Sam. 13:14).

Ego ex eorum numero me esse profiteer qui scribunt proficiendo, & scribendo proficient.
Augustine, Letters 153.2,
via Ioannes Calvinus

I

DAVID AND

BIBLICAL THEOLOGY

He stood out among the masses crowded near the Dung Gate at the south end of the Old City of Jerusalem, long blond hair and deep blue eyes, dressed in a long flowing white gown with a crown on his head and a harp in his arms. His routine was to play a few songs and then invite tourists on a guided visit of the temple mount and the Jewish quarter. This modern-day "King David" was relying on the Western image of this ancient king to try to make a living in a city filled with pilgrims. This image was one that I knew well, drawn from the Sunday school pictures and illustrated Bibles of my childhood.

At the same time at an archaeological dig in the northern part of Israel, at Tel Dan, in ancient times the northernmost city of the tribes of Israel, an astonishing find was announced to the media. Archaeologists had discovered a mid-ninth century BC stele, that is, a stone monument inscribed with letters. The letters comprised thirteen lines written in the Aramaic language, and near the center of the inscription was the phrase "house of David." The text chronicled events strikingly similar to the massacre of Joram and Ahaziah in 2 Kings 9. The ancient letters identified Ahaziah as a king from the house or dynasty of David. The inscription created a sensation because it was the oldest archaeological evidence for the existence of a dynasty that originated in a figure named David.[1]

These two events from modern-day Israel remind us at the outset of at least two images of David that exist in our world today. There is the contemporary image of David, one that has been forged through millennia of Jewish and Christian history, through ancient, medieval, and modern art, and is now painted in our collective mind's eye. At the same time there is a historical image of David, one that has been reconstructed from archaeological evidence and ancient Near Eastern texts and sifted through the scientific perspective of modern scholars. These two images, contemporary and historical, rarely coincide.

There is, however, another image of David, one that sometimes overlaps with one or the other of these two images. It is the David of the canon, that is, the literary-theological image of David in the biblical texts. Certainly there are some elements of this image of David that have informed the contemporary image of David, even if many aspects of the latter reflect inappropriate modern impositions. Certainly the canonical David is connected to the historical David, even if it is clear that there was much more to the David of history than is now recorded in the Scriptures. The goal of this book, however, is to offer you a theological portrait of the David of the Bible, rooted in his historical context and relevant to our contemporary context, expressed as a theological witness to God and his redemptive purposes in our world.

There are some who would expect and appreciate a book defending the historical David against the onslaught of recent minimalist approaches according to which David is but a literary myth.[2] But, although a legitimate exercise, this will not be the focus of this book.[3] There are others who are looking for ready-made sermons that provide quick and easy access to David for popular consumption. Although this book will show the way the canonical presentation of David can and does shape contemporary life, this will be based on a patient encounter with the biblical text which I hope will lay a foundation for a series of sermons or Bible studies.

DAVID AND NEW TESTAMENT THEOLOGY

Our journey through the Old Testament theological theme of David will begin in what for many is an unlikely place: the New Testament. By doing this we hope to provide a theological map to guide Christian readers to the scenic vistas of Old Testament theology.

There is little question that King David receives considerable attention in the pages of the New Testament. He is mentioned as a towering past figure in the great redemptive story of Israel (Matt. 1:6, 17; 12:3; 22:43, 45; Mark 2:25; 12:36–37; Acts 7:45; 13:22; Heb. 11:32). As such a past figure he is a source of authority, whether through revelation (Mark 12:36; Acts 1:16; 2:29–30; 4:25) or through example (Luke 6:3–5; Heb. 11:32). He also is identified clearly as the source of the royal line and messianic hope for Israel in the time of Jesus (Matt. 22:42; Mark 11:10; 12:35), a hope that Christ's followers identified with Jesus who was called the son of David (Matt. 1:1, 20; 9:27; 12:23; 15:22; 20:30–31; 21:9, 15; Mark 10:47–48; Luke 1:27). This preliminary evidence shows how important David was to the early Christian community. His words and example were key to the early Christian community, but in what ways were his words and example applied?

First of all, Christ is viewed as the son of David, the one who fulfilled the messianic hope, who reestablished the Davidic line. This fact is clear from the opening passage in the present form of the New Testament as Matthew 1 places the accent on Jesus' Davidic roots as well as his birth in Bethlehem, the home village of David. Such an emphasis on Jesus' Davidic roots can be seen in Romans 1:3 ("who as to his human flesh was born a descendent of David") and Hebrews 1:5 (cf. 1:8–13). Hebrews 1:5 draws heavily on Psalm 2, a psalm which trumpets the ascension of the Davidic king to the throne, and 2 Samuel 7, a passage which expresses the covenantal agreement between Yahweh and the Davidic house. This initial connection, that is, between Jesus Christ and David is obvious to most, but is easy to take for granted. It is important to realize that our appropriation of the Davidic story is possible only through and because of Christ's foundational link to David.

The second connection, however, is often overlooked by Christians. In 2 Corinthians 6:18, the apostle Paul clearly alludes to the same passage in 2 Samuel 7 that we have already seen is used elsewhere to forge a link between Jesus and David. However, in this instance there is a slight change. Whereas in 2 Samuel 7:14, the reference is "I will be his father, and he will be my son," in 2 Corinthians 6:18 Paul modifies this to "I will be a father to you, and you will be my sons and daughters." Here the apostle does two things. First, he makes the original Davidic covenantal promise plural ("sons"), indicating that he is speaking about a community. Second, he includes both male and female ("sons and daughters"), a significant declaration in an ancient patriarchal age. By doing this he is revealing that the Davidic covenant now rests upon the community of Christ as a whole, which now functions in the line of David as vice-regents of God on earth.

This is very important to our appropriation of the image and tradition of David in the Old Testament. As we encounter David in the Old Testament we need to see him as a type of the coming Messiah; the role he fills within Israel reveals the role that his messianic descendant would fulfill. On one level this is truly redemptive-historical, that is, David's role can be fulfilled only by the Christ in a unique and singular way. However, the New Testament also suggests that in and through this Christ we as a community enter into the Davidic covenant and in some way also fulfill the function of David.

The reason I want to share this at the outset of the book is to provide you with the theological framework to appropriate the Davidic image and tradition in the Old Testament for your lives as Christians. As we encounter the various aspects of this tradition, you need to first consider how this anticipates and is fulfilled in Christ. But after doing this you are compelled by the New Testament witness to reflect on the way in which the various aspects can become a reality for us who share the name Christian: that is, Messiah-ones.

These two hermeneutical movements, one redemptive-historical and the other redemptive-ethical, are echoed in the apostle Paul's encouragement to young Timothy in 2 Timothy 3:14–17 to embrace the Old Testament as normative Scripture for his Christian life and ministry. Old Testament texts are, according to Paul, "holy Scriptures, which are able to make you wise for salvation through faith in Christ Jesus," that is, they function as witness to the grand story of redemption that culminates in and through Jesus Christ, the son of David. In addition, Paul continues, these same texts ("All Scripture") which are "God-breathed" are "useful for teaching, rebuking, correcting and training in righteousness, so that all God's people may be thoroughly equipped for every good work" (TNIV), that is, they function as witness to God's grand ethic of redemption which is expressed in and through the body of Christ (the church) animated by the Spirit of Christ.

Notice how the redemptive story and ethic are drawn from "Scripture," a translation of the Greek word *graphē* which refers to the written texts of the Old Testament canon. This is key to our present theological enterprise. It is not the history reconstructed from these texts (and other sources) nor is it depictions evident in contemporary expressions from which we take our lead in this study. Rather, it is the portrait of David preserved within the canonical witness that guides our theological reflection. This authoritative witness compels us to not merely reflect, but to respond in word and deed to the David of Scripture.

DAVID AND OLD TESTAMENT THEOLOGY

Now that we have laid a foundation for our appropriation of the image of David in light of the New Testament, there is a need also to consider a foundational interpretive issue in Old Testament theology. One of the key questions that dogs the presentation of David in the Old Testament is whether kingship as an institution was a divinely initiated or divinely permitted office for Israel.[4] To this question we now turn.

Kingship after the Israelites' Hearts

Although it is not the earliest mention of kingship in the Old Testament, 1 Samuel 8 is probably the first passage to which people turn when discussing the theme of kingship. This chapter presents a scene from late in the career of the great leader Samuel. When the people approached Samuel requesting a king to lead them, the old leader was deeply disturbed and so inquired of the Lord to discern his will. The answer from God was troubling: "Listen to all that the people are saying to you; it is not you they have rejected, but they have rejected me as their king. As they have done from the day I brought them up out of Egypt until this day, forsaking me and serving other gods, so they are doing to you" (1 Sam. 8:7–8).

At first, it appears from Samuel's concern and the Lord's response that he did not regard kingship as a positive development for Israel. This suggests that when kingship became a legitimate office within Israel, it had more to do with God's permissive will than with his intentional will (he permits it, but it was not his intention). However, a closer look at the Israelites' request as well as God's response brings this preliminary conclusion into question.

In their initial request to Samuel the people request a king "such as all the other nations have" (1 Sam. 8:5). This is expanded later in the scene as they cry: "We want a king over us. Then we will be like all the other nations, with a king to lead us and to go out before us and fight our battles" (1 Sam. 8:19–20).

The circumstances of this request are described more fully in Samuel's farewell speech in 1 Samuel 12:12 as Samuel reminds them: "But when you saw that Nahash king of the Ammonites was moving against you, you said to me, 'No, we want a king to rule over us'—even though the LORD your God was your king."

These statements by the people and prophet reveal the perception of kingship in the minds of the people. Human kingship was linked to war. Tired of their vulnerability among the nations, the people wanted to experience the military security that a human king with his standing army could bring. This helps clarify God's warning to the people in 1 Samuel 8:10–18. God warns them that the kind of king they are requesting would take their children and resources in order to sustain his royal court and army.

A king in line with the wishes of the Israelites was a military leader who would offer them peace and security, and soon God would provide them with such a leader in Saul, son of Kish. He was a towering physical specimen: "an impressive young man without equal among the Israelites— a head taller than any of the others" (1 Sam. 9:2), well-suited to the military role expected by the Israelites.

God's Kingship

God's offense at the Israelites' request for a military king can only be understood in light of the greatest salvation event in Israel's history. In Exodus 12–14 the Lord delivers his people from Egypt by parting the waters of the sea and then defeats their enemy by returning the waters to their normal course. This momentous victory is celebrated in Exodus 15 in the ancient song of praise sung by Moses and the Israelites (Ex. 15:1–18).

The song begins by accentuating the battle prowess of the Lord God, exalting him as the "warrior" who "has hurled into the sea" Pharaoh and his men. The language is that of a military victory with reference to "horse," "rider," "chariots," "army," and "officers." The ending of the song, however, identifies the implications of this great victory in war as the celebrants cry: "the LORD will reign for ever and ever." This battle is a declaration to all peoples, whether Egypt whence they have come or Canaan to which they are going (Edom, Moab, Canaan, v. 15) that the Lord is King of kings, Lord of lords, and that there is none among the gods like Yahweh. The passage looks to the day when God will take up his residence in his divine palace, the temple in Jerusalem (15:13, 17) from where Yahweh will reign forever. Therefore, this great victory in battle is foundational to God's claim of kingship.

God's kingship over Israel as a nation was demonstrated through his defeat of Egypt and defense of Israel at the sea. In this event Israel did not have to raise a spear or sword; God was their warrior. This was to be a defining moment for Israel: God was their king because God was their warrior who would fight for them. Even when the Israelites were instructed to participate in war, God was careful to remind them that victory was accomplished only through reliance upon God their warrior. In Exodus 17:8–16 it is Moses' reliance upon God on the hill above the battle scene that secures victory. The account in Exodus 17 makes it clear that Joshua must know the divine source of this victory; thus the Lord tells Moses: "Write this on a scroll as something to be remembered and make sure that Joshua hears it, because I will completely blot out the memory of

Amalek from under heaven" (17:14). This is an important truth for Joshua to know, since he would be the one who would lead Israel in the conquest of the Promised Land.

Therefore, in light of the fact that military protection was the key prerogative of kingship within Israel, one can understand why kingship and battle were linked in the minds of the Israelites and why their request was interpreted as a rejection of God's kingship in the heavenly realms. Nevertheless, does this mean that kingship per se was unacceptable to God?

Expectation of Kingship

To answer this we need to look further afield. The biblical witness does not present kingship as a late-breaking emphasis in the twilight years of Samuel's ministry. According to Genesis 17 the covenant ceremony between God and Abraham included the promise that "kings will come from you" (17:6). This promise is made more specific later in Genesis as Jacob blesses his sons, for as he addresses Judah, the old man declares: "the scepter will not depart from Judah, nor the ruler's staff from between his feet, until he comes to whom it belongs and the obedience of the nations is his" (Gen. 49:10). Using images well known from Egyptian Pharaohs (scepter/staff), the patriarch presages that a king would come forth from the tribe of Judah and that this king would rule not only over the nations, but also over "your father's sons" (Gen. 49:8).

The book of Deuteronomy depicts the final speech of Moses to a people poised to conquer the land of Canaan. The role of a king presupposed by this scene is true not only on the historical level, but also on the literary level as it represents the final installment of the Torah, but also the introduction to the story of Israel that stretches from Joshua through 2 Kings and is often called the "Deuteronomic History," the story of Israel described through the lens of Deuteronomy. The book of Deuteronomy itself assumes the appointment of a king once the people had settled in the land (Deut. 17:14–20). This future appointment is expressed in ways that reveal their affinity with the stories related in Samuel, highlighting the people's request for a king. The reference to the appointment of the king here is depicted in descriptive rather than prescriptive terms, that is, God speaks of the time when the people would ask for a king and offers his guidance on how the king should act, but does not say whether kingship is his preferred modus operandi.

This, however, becomes clearer in the book of Judges. At the core of this fascinating book is the account of a series of twelve judges whom God raised up in the years between the death of Joshua and the birth of Samuel. Significant emphasis is placed on six of these judges (Othniel, Ehud, Deborah, Gideon, Jephthah, and Samson),[5] while six are mentioned only in passing (Shamgar, Tola, Jair, Ibzan, Elon, Abdon). These judges were empowered by the "spirit of the Lord" (e.g., Jephthah, 11:29) and accomplished mighty deeds.

These stories press home two key principles. First, the people of God are prone to idolatry and sin as can be seen in the repeating cycle of sin (peace-disobedience-discipline-cry-salvation-peace; see, e.g., Judg. 2:10–23). Second, God must raise up leadership on a regular basis to rescue his people. The first three major accounts of these judges (Othniel, Ehud, Deborah) are largely positive. But as the narrative progresses, the leaders commit grave errors of judgment: Gideon is mighty, but after obediently destroying the Asherah pole in his hometown and refusing Israel's desire for military kingship ("The LORD will rule over you," 8:22–23), he makes a trap for his own people with his ephod. Abimelech tries to become king and it ends in disaster (Judg. 9). Jephthah spoils his story by sacrificing his daughter to the Lord (Judg. 10:6–12:7). Finally, Samson, who begins with such promise, represents the greatest tragedy of the entire series of judges (Judg. 13–16). Thus these stories of judges depict a rebellious people, but also an inconsistent leadership structure.

Although Samson is the final judge in the book, his story is not the conclusion to the book. Rather there are five more chapters, and in these chapters we are given some of the most shocking stories in the Old Testament. In chapters 17–18 we are told the story of Micah's idols, and in chapters 19–21, the story of the rape and murder of the Levite's concubine and near demise of the tribe of Benjamin. While in Judges 2–16 there is little focus on the tribal identity of the various characters and events, in chapters 17–21 tribal identity is emphasized. These chapters present a picture of the tribes of Israel in disunity, destroying one another.

At the beginning and ending of this section of the book is found what is probably the most famous phrase from the book: "In those days Israel had no king; everyone did as they saw fit" (17:6 TNIV; 21:25; cf. 18:1; 19:1). Many consider the clause "everyone did as they saw fit" as a picture of moral anarchy and relativism: all did as they saw fit, creating standards for themselves and rejecting God's Torah standards. The only other place in the Bible that this phrase appears is in Deuteronomy 12. After reviewing the various ways that the Canaanites worshiped their gods in the land, the people are commanded:

> You must not worship the LORD your God in their way. But you are to seek the place the LORD your God will choose from among all your tribes to put his Name [shem] there [sham] for his dwelling. To that place [sham] you must go; there [sham] bring your burnt offerings and sacrifices, your tithes and special gifts, what you have vowed to give and your freewill offerings, and the firstborn of your herds and flocks. There [sham], in the presence of the LORD

your God, you and your families shall eat and shall rejoice in everything you have put your hand to, because the LORD your God has blessed you.

You are not to do as we do here today, everyone doing as they see fit, since you have not yet reached the resting place and the inheritance the LORD your God is giving you. But you will cross the Jordan and settle in the land the LORD your God is giving you as an inheritance, and he will give you rest from all your enemies around you so that you will live in safety. Then to the place the LORD your God will choose as a dwelling for his Name [*shem*]—there [*sham*, 2x] you are to bring everything I command you: your burnt offerings and sacrifices, your tithes and special gifts, and all the choice possessions you have vowed to the LORD. And there rejoice before the LORD your God—you, your sons and daughters, your male and female servants, and the Levites from your towns who have no allotment or inheritance of their own. Be careful not to sacrifice your burnt offerings anywhere you please. Offer them only at the place the LORD will choose in one of your tribes, and there [*sham*] observe everything I command you. (Deut. 12:4–14 TNIV)

This speech refers to the worship of the people and the call of God to centralize their worship in one place once they enter the land. But in Judges all did as they saw fit, continuing the practice in the wilderness which left them vulnerable to the idolatrous practices of the Canaanites who preceded them and were judged. The Israelites were worshiping God in their own ways, at their own places. But God had instructed them to fix a central place for their worship.

The clause "everyone did as they saw fit" is linked to another key clause in Judges: "in those days Israel had no king." Some have suggested that the reference here is to God's kingship, that is, "in those days Israel did not submit to God as their king." However, several lines of evidence suggest that the narrator is referring to a human king and that this king was none other than David and his dynasty in contrast to Saul.

First of all, the issue of worship in the story of Micah (chs. 17–18) is related to the establishment of the cult center of the Northern Kingdom which split away from the southern Davidic kingdom (18:28–31). Second, the issue of injustice in the story of Benjamin's demise (chs. 19–21) is related not only to the tribe of Benjamin (which was the tribe of Saul), but to the town of Gibeah (the precise village from which Saul came). Third, in both of these stories the other key characters involve the tribes of Ephraim and the clan of Bethlehem in Judah (Micah was from Ephraim and hires a young Levite from Bethlehem in Judah, a Levite from Ephraim took a concubine from Bethlehem in Judah and that Bethlehemite woman is killed). Fourth, clearly Saul's family power base was in Benjamin and then extended beyond this to the northern tribes, the very negative characters in these two stories at the end of Judges. Fifth, when the tribes of Israel inquire of God in Judges 20:18 as to who should go up first to fight against Benjamin, the answer is that Judah should go up first, identifying Judah as the leadership tribe for Israel. This identification of Judah as the leader of Israel is also seen in Judges 1:1–21; as the tribes consider fighting against an enemy after the death of Joshua, Judah is identified as the tribe which would initiate the battle.[6]

Given the evidence from the central "judges" section of this book, evidence that shows the ineffectiveness of leadership through judges, together with the evidence from the final chapters (16–21), the book appears to be encouraging a form of kingship that facilitates the command of Moses in Deuteronomy 12. Negative depictions of the tribe of Benjamin and in particular the clan of Gibeah, and positive depictions of the tribe of Judah and the victimization of Bethlehemites, suggest that David is in view as the king who would accomplish unification of the tribes.

Some might suggest that kingship, however, does not receive positive exposure in the "judges" section of the book. The people approach Gideon to establish a dynasty (Judg. 8:22–23) and are rebuffed, for "the Lord will rule over you." The Abimelech story which follows Gideon's death shows the disaster of an experiment in kingship. However, a closer look reveals that the people's request for a king in Judges 8:22 echoes the same problem found in Israel's request for a king in 1 Samuel: "because you have saved us out of the hand of Midian." Their motivation for kingship was to take away from the Lord his divine prerogatives. The story of Abimelech does not necessarily disqualify kingship, but rather disqualifies kingship gained and retained in the wrong way (that is, through human initiative and shedding of blood).

Thus the book of Judges longs for a king from the tribe of Judah who would unify and lead Israel. Until that happened the kinds of stories found in Judges would endure, stories of idolatry, disunity, and liaisons with the Canaanites.

The books of Samuel and Kings catalogue the failures of the Davidic kings, even if several figures do fulfill the calling of sustaining worship and purity (esp. Hezekiah, 2 Kings 18–20, and Josiah, 2 Kings 22–23). In the end, however, the royal house fails and Judah is destroyed and many of its people exiled. The writer of Kings, however, does not even then disqualify the Davidic dynasty, but ends his book with the account of Jehoiachin's release from prison in Babylon (2 Kings 25:27–30), a sign of hope for the renewal of the Davidic line to its rightful place.

The evidence that we have highlighted in the Torah and the Former Prophets (Genesis–2 Kings) reveals that there were an expectation and justification for some form of royal rule in Israel, and that such was not an afterthought or even an accommodation to human sinfulness. This fixation with kingship and the Davidic dynasty will be affirmed in our final chapter ("David and Messiah") as we look at the witness of the Latter Prophets (Isaiah–Malachi). Therefore, God's problem with kingship in 1 Samuel is not with the royal office per se, but rather with the Israelite conception of kingship, especially their intention to switch their reliance and allegiance from divine to human king.

FOR FURTHER REFLECTION

1. As you begin this study reflect honestly on the image of David that is present in your mind. Ask a close friend or family member to do the same and discuss the source of your image.

2. Describe how you think Christians should approach and appropriate the Old Testament. Is it Christian Scripture? Is it foundational to Christian Scripture? Does it have enduring relevance to us today? Why?

3. What is the relationship between history and theology? Is it important that David lived in historical time and space? Why?

4. We have distinguished between "redemptive-historical" and "redemptive-ethical" in this chapter. Can you distinguish between these two ways in which the Old Testament is related to us as Christians? Give examples of truth in the Old Testament that is one or the other.

5. Is it essential that kingship be the intentional design of God? Why?

6. For God to be king meant that Israel would have to be passive, entrusting themselves into the hands of their Divine Warrior. What challenges do you face in which you need to entrust yourself into the hands of God?

2

DAVID, ABRAHAM, AND RUTH

I n the previous chapter we looked at the pervasiveness of the expectation and exaltation of Davidic kingship in the Old and New Testaments. In this chapter we will focus on one particular (and tiny) book in the Old Testament that reveals God's faithfulness to raise up and preserve David and his dynasty in order that the fundamental promises to Abraham would be fulfilled not only for his people, but also for all the nations of the earth.

ABRAHAM

It is clear that the Abrahamic tradition is foundational for Israel's identity as a people. The most extensive expression of this tradition in the Old Testament is now found in a narrative block that is entitled the "generations" (*toledoth*) of Terah (Abraham's father) and stretches from Genesis 11:27 to 25:11.

Key to this Abrahamic account is a series of encounters between God and Abraham that initiate and solidify their covenant relationship (Gen. 12, 15, 17). Common to each of these encounters is the repetition of the two core promises of God to Abraham.

The LORD had said to Abram, "Leave your country, your people and your father's household and go to the land I will show you.

> I will make you into a great nation
>> and I will bless you;
> I will make your name great,
>> and you will be a blessing." (Gen. 12:1–2)

The LORD appeared to Abram and said, "To your offspring I will give this land." (Gen. 12:7)

The LORD said to Abram after Lot had parted from him, "Lift up your eyes from where you are and look north and south, east and west. All the land that you see I will give to you and your offspring forever. I will make your offspring like the dust of the earth, so that if anyone could count the dust, then your offspring could be counted. Go, walk through the length and breadth of the land, for I am giving it to you." (Gen. 13:14–17)

Then the word of the LORD came to him: "This man will not be your heir, but a son coming from your own body will be your heir." He took him outside and said, "Look up at the heavens and count the stars—if indeed you can count them." Then he said to him, "So shall your offspring be."

Abram believed the LORD, and he credited it to him as righteousness.

He also said to him, "I am the LORD, who brought you out of Ur of the Chaldeans to give you this land to take possession of it." (Gen. 15:4–7)

On that day the LORD made a covenant with Abram and said, "To your descendants I give this land, from the river of Egypt to the great river, the Euphrates." (Gen. 15:18)

Abram fell facedown, and God said to him, "As for me, this is my covenant with you: You will be the father of many nations. No longer will you be called Abram; your name will be Abraham, for I have made you a father of many nations. I will make you very fruitful; I will make nations of you, and kings will come from you. I will establish my covenant as an everlasting covenant between me and you and your descendants after you for the generations to come, to be your God and the God of your descendants after you. The whole land of Canaan, where you are now an alien, I will give as an everlasting possession to you and your descendants after you; and I will be their God." (Gen. 17:3–8)

In each of these divine declarations God makes two promises. First, the Lord promises Abraham countless seed, a family that would grow into a great nation. Throughout the Abrahamic account this promise is under constant threat, exemplified by several crises including barrenness (Gen. 15:2–3; 16:1; 29:31; 30:1), death (Gen. 22), loss of seed-bearer (Gen. 12:10–20; 20:1–18; 26:1–35), and threat to the purity of the line (Gen. 26:34–35; 38:1–30).[1] Second, God promises Abraham a vast land, essential for supporting this large nation. The fulfillment of this promise is never in sight throughout Abraham's life as he and his family wander throughout the land of Canaan, acquiring nothing more than a burial site in this land (Gen. 23).

These two promises of seed and land to Abraham echo the dual themes of earlier promises to humanity in Genesis 1:28 ("God blessed them and said to them, 'Be fruitful and increase in number; fill the earth and subdue it'") and Genesis 9:1 ("Then God blessed Noah and his sons, saying to them, 'Be fruitful and increase in number and fill the earth'"; cf. 9:7), and confirm Abraham's status as the founder of a new humanity, a redemptive clan through which God would bring blessing to "all peoples on earth" (Gen. 12:3).

These two promises (seed, land) also shape much of what is to come in the grand redemptive story of the Old Testament and will be repeated at key junctures, for instance, as God begins the great rescue of the exodus (Ex. 6:1–9), as Moses charges the people poised for conquest (Deut. 6:1–9), or as God makes covenant with David in Jerusalem (2 Sam. 7:10–16). So also, it is these two promises that underlie one of the most memorable stories found in the Old Testament, the story recounted in the book of Ruth, a story that traces the roots of David's participation in the grand story of redemption in the Old Testament.

RUTH

The book of Ruth, set in the time of the judges (Ruth 1:1), begins with a contrast between these two fundamental promises. The land is unable to fulfill its role of sustaining the promised seed as a man named Elimelech, his wife Naomi, and their two sons Mahlon and Kilion must flee from their hometown in Bethlehem of Judah to the land of Moab (1:1). The irony of this crisis is that Bethlehem, which in Hebrew means "house" (*beth*) of "bread" (*lehem*), is unable to provide the necessary seed (grain) to sustain the seed (human) promised to Abraham. The crisis in the promise of land, however, soon spreads to crisis in the promise of seed (human) as first Elimelech and then his two sons die in the land of Moab, leaving the family without heirs (1:3–5).

It is at this point in the story that we are told that the widowed and childless Naomi learns that "the LORD had come to the aid of his people by providing food (*lehem*) for them" (1:6), and it is this news that prompts her return to the land of Judah, to the newly blessed house of bread

(*Beth-lehem*). Unlike her sister-in-law Orpah, the persistent Ruth refuses to abandon her mother-in-law,[2] even though Naomi emphasizes the fact that she cannot offer another son (seed) to support her. Ruth accompanies Naomi on the road to Bethlehem (1:18–19).

The scene at the entrance to the town of Bethlehem is one of the most dramatic in the Old Testament, assembling Naomi, Ruth, and the women of Bethlehem to record the depth of bitterness of this woman who has endured much loss (1:19–21). The grieving mother and wife refuses to be called by her name Naomi ("pleasant"), choosing rather Mara ("bitter") because, as she exclaims, "I went away full, but the LORD has brought me back empty" (1:21). At this critical juncture in the story Naomi reminds us of the crisis in the promise of seed, a crisis that seemed to parallel a crisis in the promise of land (famine). Then the narrator of Ruth makes what appears to be a simple summarizing statement: "So Naomi returned from Moab accompanied by Ruth the Moabitess, her daughter-in-law, arriving in Bethlehem as the barley harvest was beginning" (1:22). This statement, however, is loaded with metaphorical significance. This woman, who left a land without seed (grain) and ultimately lost her seed (human), hears of God's grace in the land through seed (grain) and so returns. As she enters into this land seedless (human), all around her are signs of God's grace in the seed (grain) being harvested by the people of Bethlehem. It is in the midst of this harvest of the seed of the land that the drama of God's provision of the promise of human seed will be accomplished.

Having lost their only source of income in their ancient patriarchal economy (that is, husbands), Naomi and Ruth must rely upon ancient forms of welfare, and the story of Ruth introduces us to the ancient provision that allowed the poor to gather any grain which was missed by harvesters (cf. Lev. 19:9–10: 23:22; Deut. 24:19–22). In order to do this, the younger woman Ruth went out to the harvest fields surrounding Bethlehem and into the field of Naomi's relative Boaz. There she not only was allowed to glean, but was welcomed by Boaz to remain in his field, to drink from his water jars, and to eat with his workers. Boaz ensures her protection in his field (2:9) and guarantees that her gleaning efforts will be richly rewarded by having his men leave behind plenty of unharvested grain (2:15–16). Here we see how the promise of land was used to keep alive the promise of seed, that is, the practice of gleaning ensured the physical survival of Naomi and the seed-bearer Ruth.

The metaphorical character of this scene, however, should not be missed. At lunchtime Boaz not only offers her bread and wine, but also some roasted grain which she eats to her fill with some left over. Her gleaning efforts yield an ephah of grain and this she brings home along with the leftover roasted grain to her mother-in-law. This picture of Boaz's seed (grain) being relayed through Ruth to Naomi not only intertwines the promises of seed and land, but also foreshadows the ultimate outcome of the story when Boaz's seed (human) will be relayed through Ruth to Naomi in the form of the child Obed (Ruth 4).

This intermixing of seed and land continues into the third chapter of the book as Ruth embarks on the most daring action of the plot. This action is prompted by Naomi who sends her with the intention to prompt a union between Boaz and Ruth. The scene takes place at Boaz's threshing floor, a scene filled with the image of seed freshly harvested from the fields of Ruth 2. Approaching the "good-spirited" Boaz, lying down to rest "at the far end of the grain pile," Ruth broaches the subject of a conjugal union with the invitation to "spread the corner of your garment over me, since you are a kinsman-redeemer" (3:9). Boaz, however, is aware of another closer relative who is first in line to fulfill the role of kinsman-redeemer and promises to tackle the issue straightaway the following day. Almost as a down payment to ensure his word, he offers Ruth six measures of barley to carry back to her mother-in-law. The picture of Ruth again carrying barley seed from Boaz to her mother-in-law enhances the foreshadowing of the ultimate resolution of this story.

The plot is finally resolved in Ruth 4 as Boaz fulfills his promise to settle the matter. To do this would demand a careful handling of ancient crisis customs. In Ruth 2 Boaz displayed his knowledge of and dedication to the ancient crisis custom of gleaning. Now in Ruth 4 Boaz displays his brilliance in leveraging other ancient crisis customs to carefully defend the two widows' interests.

These two crisis customs are reflected in the Hebrew legal code. Although the precise relationship between the form of the customs in Ruth 4 and the laws encased in the Torah is difficult to ascertain, a review of the traditions in the legal code provides helpful background.

The first law is often called the law of the kinsman-redeemer. The land was apportioned to the tribes of Israel, clan by clan and family by family, with the understanding that the tribal and clan boundaries of the land would remain static throughout the history of Israel. However, there was a provision for Israelites to lease their land in times of severe economic crisis with the understanding that at the year of jubilee (every fiftieth year) the land would revert back to the original owner. If land was "leased" due to economic hardship, however, there were terms in the law for the land to be "redeemed" by a person called a *go'el*, that is, a kinsman-redeemer, one who was willing to pay the lessee to revert the land back to the original family prior to the year of jubilee (Lev. 25:23–28).[3]

The second law is usually called the "levirate marriage" law. It was important to the Israelites that each family, clan, and tribe endure within the nation, but as is evident throughout the stories of Israel (Sarah, Rachel, Hannah), barrenness was a reality for some families. To provide for an enduring line, the law regulated what was called levirate marriage (Deut 25:5–10). If a man died without an heir to carry on his family line, his brother was required to produce an heir with the dead man's widow.

In the Torah these laws are never linked so clearly as they are in the book of Ruth. In Ruth 3:9 Ruth herself unites the issues of marriage and land when she declares: "Spread the corner of your garment over me, since you are a kinsman-redeemer." In Ruth 4:1–5, Boaz confronts the unnamed closest relative with the challenge to first buy the land, but then immediately links the purchase of the land (kinsman-redeemer custom) with the production of a child through the dead man's widow (levirate marriage custom): "On the day you buy the land from Naomi and from Ruth the Moabitess, you acquire the dead man's widow, in order to maintain the name of the dead with his property" (4:5). When the closest relative balks at this demand, inviting Boaz to take his place, Boaz's announcement again links the two customs: "Today you are witnesses that I have bought from Naomi all the property of Elimelech, Kilion and Mahlon. I have also acquired Ruth the Moabitess, Mahlon's widow, as my wife, in order to maintain the name of the dead with his property, so that his name will not disappear from among his family or from the town records. Today you are witnesses!" (4:9–10).

This fascinating interweaving of the two customs emphasizes again the intricate relationship between the promises of land and seed in the book of Ruth, for the one custom regulates the enduring promise of land and the other the enduring promise of seed. By intertwining the two customs we see again how the promise of land is used to sustain the promise of seed.

The final scene of the book of Ruth reveals the outcome of the intricate plot presented in earlier chapters (4:13–17). Ruth becomes Boaz's wife and together they produce a child. At this point there is an echo of an earlier scene in Ruth 1 where Naomi, Ruth, and the women of Bethlehem are assembled at the gate of Bethlehem. It is Naomi, however, rather than Ruth who becomes the reference point for the child. He is Naomi's kinsman-redeemer, and he is given into Naomi's care and called her son. The one who went away full and returned empty (1:21) is now full again. As we have intimated already, this transference of seed from Boaz through Ruth to Naomi has been foreshadowed in two earlier scenes in this book as seed from Boaz's field was given to Ruth for Naomi.

In the creative intertwining of the motifs of land and seed, human and harvest seed, it is evident that the priority is placed ultimately on the production of human seed, the fulfillment of the promise of enduring offspring for the people of God. The narrative proper does not end with this little kinsman-redeemer, Obed. Rather we are told that Obed was the father of Jesse who in turn was the father of David. To this has been added a genealogical appendix which also ends with the name of David. The book of Ruth, thus, is ultimately not even a story about Ruth, Boaz, or Naomi, but about God's providential care for the family that would bring forth David and ultimately the Messiah in his line. Throughout the story, this providential care is consistently expressed through the covenant faithfulness of Ruth (2:11; 3:10) and Boaz (2:12–13, 20) to Naomi. As we will see, this quality of covenant faithfulness will also be displayed by David (see ch. 11: "David and Faithfulness").

David thus represents the seed who will truly provide a secure land for Israel as a nation. This is made explicit in God's speech to David in 2 Samuel 7:12 when God promises to David seed with a land: "When your days are over and you rest with your fathers, I will raise up your offspring to succeed you, who will come from your own body, and I will establish his kingdom." The purpose of this dynasty is made explicit in 7:10: "And I will provide a place for my people Israel and will plant them so that they can have a home of their own and no longer be disturbed."

The promise of seed and land finds its initial fulfillment in the books of Genesis–Joshua. However, the crisis of the book of Judges reveals the need for a form of leadership that would secure these promises for the people of God. It is fascinating that the book of Ruth highlights these two promises in this period of crisis, introducing this family that would be so instrumental in securing land and seed for the people of God.

IMPLICATIONS

The story of Ruth is not forgotten in the annals of God's people. At the outset of the New Testament the gospel of Matthew includes Ruth in its genealogy of Jesus, the son of David, the son of Abraham. Along with her are three other women (Tamar, Rahab, Bathsheba), all of whom stand out in the long list, not only because of their gender, but also because of the fact that all are described as women with questionable sexual histories.[4] These names are included in this genealogy to bring into view their four stories, which in turn set up a fifth story that begins the narrative of the gospel of Matthew, that is, the story of another woman whose sexual chastity was brought into question, but for whom God faithfully provided a means by which she and her child would be legitimated within the community of God. This child, the last in the long genealogy, was the ultimate child of promise, the Messiah, the Christ.

The story of Ruth, therefore, ultimately finds its fulfillment and significance not merely in the person of David and his dynasty, but in the Davidic son Jesus. And through

Jesus, the son of David, the son of Abraham (Matt. 1:1), the promises to Abraham are fulfilled.

The fulfillment of these promises, however, as suggested by the presence of four Gentile women in Jesus' genealogy,[5] is not merely for Israel, but, as God intended in Genesis 12:1–3, for the blessing of all nations, a purpose of the Davidic kings (Ps. 72:17b) and of Jesus the Messiah (Gal. 3:8, 14; cf. Acts 3:25; Rom. 4:16–17).

> I will bless those who bless you,
>   and whoever curses you I will curse;
> and all peoples on earth
>   will be blessed through you. (Gen. 12:3)

> All nations will be blessed through him,
>   and they will call him blessed. (Ps. 72:17b)

> The Scripture foresaw that God would justify the Gentiles by faith, and announced the gospel in advance to Abraham: "All nations will be blessed through you." . . . He redeemed us in order that the blessing given to Abraham might come to the Gentiles through Christ Jesus, so that by faith we might receive the promise of the Spirit. (Gal. 3:8, 14)

As Christians reflect on this grand story of redemption begun in Abraham, enduring through the fragile scenes in the book of Ruth, continuing through the reign of David, and finding its ultimate expression in the death, resurrection, and ascension of his son Jesus, they are drawn to praise and glory in the God of providence and grace. Additionally, this international context for the promises given to Abraham long ago, enduring because of the foreigner Ruth, secured in David, and ultimately fulfilled in Christ, is what propels the community of the Messiah to proclaim the message of this blessing to the far corners of the earth.

FOR FURTHER REFLECTION

1. Read through the Abrahamic account in Genesis, and for each story identify the purpose for its inclusion in Genesis based on either the promise of seed or land.

2. In this chapter I mention three other women besides Ruth who appear in the genealogy of Jesus in Matthew: Tamar (Gen. 38), Rahab (Josh. 2; 6:17, 22–25), Bathsheba (2 Sam. 11). I hope you have had a chance to read these stories and notice common motifs as noted in this chapter. But you should also notice an interesting link between three stories in the Old Testament: Judah and Tamar (Gen. 38), Lot and his daughters (Gen. 13; 19:30–38), and Boaz and Ruth. Don't forget that the offspring of Judah and Tamar is the ancestor of Boaz and the offspring of Lot and his daughters is the ancestor of Ruth. Is the book of Ruth the story of the redemption of the past of two families?[6]

3. Reflect on the two scenes of women that I noted in this chapter (Ruth 1:19–21; 4:14–17). Notice the irony that Naomi and Ruth return to Bethlehem with such great need, pitied by the women of the town. They stand as sentinels of the town of Bethlehem signaling the return of the suffering member into their midst. And the town will rise to the challenge, expressing covenant faithfulness to these women through Boaz. And yet in the end is it not ironic that these two suffering women will bring even greater blessing to the town through the gift of a mighty king and dynasty who will rule the nation. Identify suffering people who have entered or are entering into your life or the life of your community to whom you have the opportunity to express covenant faithfulness. Be reminded

that they may bring greater blessing to you than you to them.

4. I once heard a sermon that contrasted Boaz and the kinsman-redeemer as the contrast between Christ and the law. What is wrong with the logic of this sermon?

5. We know from the first appearance of Boaz that this man will be the source of hope for these two women: "Just then Boaz arrived from Bethlehem and greeted the harvesters, 'The LORD be with you!' 'The LORD bless you!' they called back" (Ruth 2:4). Boaz had only a small tract of land in the clan of Ephrathah, in the tribe of Judah, in the nation of Israel, and yet he made his land a place where God's kingdom principles reigned supreme, something seen in his greeting ("the LORD be with you"), but also in his actions throughout these chapters. What is your "small tract of land" in which God has placed you? What does it mean for you to live out his kingdom principles in word and deed?

6. In light of this chapter, in what way do the promises of Abraham contain the kernel of the gospel?

3

DAVID AND ANOINTING

The Old Testament accentuates the fact that David had no part in engineering his own rise to power. This emphasis is often recognized in the account of Saul's pursuit of David, during which David is given ample opportunity to eliminate Saul and seize the throne (see ch. 11: "David and Faithfulness"). But it is often forgotten that David's initial entrance onto the national stage of Israel in 1 Samuel 16 underscores David's passivity and God's initiative in his ascension to the throne. It is to this event that we now turn.

APPOINTMENT

From its outset the book of 1 Samuel is focused on the issue of kingship. The story of God's provision of Samuel to the barren Hannah reaches its climax with her prayer of thanksgiving in chapter 2, and this prayer in turn ends on a distinctly royal note:

> He [the LORD] will give strength to his king
>   and exalt the horn of his anointed. (1 Sam. 2:10)

Thus, from the beginning Samuel's destiny is inseparable from that of the Israelite monarchy as he is used to transition the nation from a tribal confederacy rescued by charismatic judges (Judg. 2–16) to a centralized monarchy led by dynastic kings (1 Sam. 13:13; 2 Sam. 7:11–16). In this transition Samuel's role would be multifaceted as he functioned as prophet (1 Sam. 7:2–4; cf. 1 Sam. 3), priest (1 Sam. 7:5–10), and judge (1 Sam. 7:6b, 15–17). Only such a figure could command the respect of the nation to play the role of kingmaker.

The process of appointment to the royal office in Israel which Samuel will guide appears to have had two basic dimensions: one private and the other public. The private dimension was first in priority and focused on divine appointment, a commission delivered through Samuel to the individual, while the public followed the private dimension and focused on the communal recognition and acceptance of the individual as leader.

For both Saul and David the private divine dimension entailed the physical symbol of anointing with oil (1 Sam. 10:1; 1 Sam. 16:13) accompanied then by the endowment of the Spirit of God (1 Sam. 10:9–13; 1 Sam 16:13). Similarly for both royal figures the public communal dimension involved the performance of a great military exploit (1 Sam. 11:1–11; 17) followed by the public confirmation of kingship (1 Sam. 11:12–13; 2 Sam. 2:1–7; 5:1–5).

ANOINTING

First Samuel 16:1–13 thus provides the account of David's anointing to kingship. As the narrative in 1 Samuel makes clear, in contrast to Saul's quick rise to the monarchy, David's appointment would be a drawn-out affair, with a long interval between his initial private anointing and his public confirmation. Among other things, this elongated transition would serve to highlight the contrast between the figures of Saul and David, revealing ultimately the legitimacy of David as the royal of God's choosing.

The beginning of the account of David's anointing is overshadowed by the dark figure of Saul as God cuts short Samuel's mourning over the divine rejection of Israel's first king (cf. 1 Sam. 15:35). God signals the beginning of a new era by instructing Samuel to fill his horn with oil and go to the family of Jesse in Bethlehem to anoint one of his sons whom God had chosen as king.

Anointing with oil is attested throughout the Old Testament as a sign of God's consecration. Objects (altars, vessels) as well as buildings (tabernacle, temple) were set apart for divine use through ceremonial rituals that included anointing with oil (Gen. 28:18; Ex. 30:26; 40:9–15; Lev. 8:10–11; Num. 7:1). So also people were consecrated for divine service through an anointing ceremony, the most common recipients of oil being royal (e.g., 1 Sam. 10:1; 1 Kings 1:34, 39, 45) and priestly figures (e.g., Ex. 28:41; 29:7, 29; 30:30; 40:13, 15), but at least on one occasion also a prophetic figure (1 Kings 19:16; cf. Ps. 105:15// 1 Chron. 16:22; Isa. 61:1).

The significance of anointing with oil is not stated explicitly in the Old Testament. The close association between oil and celebration may be related to the use of perfumed oils which were important in an ancient society to cover up the odor of the body in a hot climate (Ruth 3:3; 2 Sam. 12:20; Pss. 23:5; 45:7; Isa. 61:3; cf. 2 Sam. 14:2; Dan. 10:3). Psalm 133, however, suggests that the act of anointing with oil in consecration is related to the blessing of God upon the individual and those he represented. It may be that oil was a valuable component of Israel's agricultural economy and thus it signified God's bountiful supply in the harvest. The fact that it could be spread over the head and even drip down the face and beard, may have reminded the Israelites of the divine blessing of rain from heaven.

DIVINE ELECTION

No matter the more general significance, in 1 Samuel 16:1–3 anointing with oil is clearly used as a sign of God's election of a particular person to serve as king over Israel. Samuel is to take his horn filled with oil to Bethlehem because God had chosen one of Jesse's sons as king to replace the rejected Saul. This time God's royal choice is unrelated to Israel's desire for a king (1 Sam. 9:20) and the stark contrast is accentuated by Samuel's initial response to Jesse's sons.

When the family arrived, the prophet was drawn immediately to the eldest son, Eliab, whose appearance and height were superior to all the sons. Samuel thought, "Surely the LORD's anointed stands here before the LORD" (1 Sam. 16:6). But Samuel, who appears to have adopted the Israelite conception of kingship at this point (see ch. 1: "David and Biblical Theology"), was rebuked by the Lord, who reminded his spokesman that the divine priority is on inner disposition ("heart") rather than outward appearance ("height"). The divinely sanctioned royal will not be a figure, as in other nations, with the towering stature of a warrior-king, but rather one whose heart is attuned to the priorities of God.

Son after son passes before Samuel, but none are chosen. As is well known, it is the insignificant youngest, whose presence was not even considered necessary by a father who also had embraced the Israelites' conception of kingship, who is chosen by the Lord to replace Saul. Samuel rises with his horn of oil and anoints the boy, signifying God's election and blessing.

DIVINE ENDOWMENT

The anointing is closely associated not only with divine election in this passage, but also with divine empowerment, for we read: "from that day on the Spirit of the LORD came upon David in power." This same concept is also expressed in the phrase "the LORD is/was with David" at several points in the books of Samuel (1 Sam. 16:18; 18:12, 14, 28; 2 Sam. 7:3). The Spirit of the Lord was associated with the appointment and function of covenant leadership figures in the Old Testament. The Spirit set apart figures like Moses and Joshua for leadership in Israel; so also the judges of Israel were clothed with the Spirit as they led the tribes into battle against their enemies (Judg. 3:10; 6:34; 11:29; 13:25; 14:6, 19; 15:14). Prophets were also closely associated with the Spirit of God (Num. 11:29; 1 Sam. 10:10; 19:20; Neh. 9:30).

That the endowment of the Spirit is restricted to David's royal function can be discerned in 1 Samuel 16:13–14. While in 1 Samuel 16:13 we are told that the "Spirit of the LORD came upon David in power," in the immediately following verse we are told that "the Spirit of the LORD had departed from Saul." This indicates that the Spirit which had been upon Saul had been transferred to David, confirming that David was now the anointed royal figure.[1] This transfer is also reflected in the claim of 1 Samuel 18:12: "the LORD was with David but had left Saul." As Moses and Joshua, the judges and prophets, so now David would be sustained and empowered by God's Spirit to lead and challenge the people (see further on Spirit-empowerment for justice in ch. 7, "David and Justice").

IMPLICATIONS

God's anointing signifies the divine election and empowerment that set apart David as the blessed royal figure for the people of God. The terms associated with this anointing, *mashah* (to anoint) and *mashiah* (anointed one), would provide the vocabulary in future generations to denote the expectations of Israel for a future ideal figure, that is, a Messiah.[2] It is this expectation that dominates the New Testament depiction of Jesus, displayed in the regular collocation "Jesus Christ" (Jesus the Messiah).

Jesus is not officially anointed with oil, but reminiscences of the ancient anointing ceremony can be discerned at his baptism when the Holy Spirit descends upon him as a dove and the voice of God declares the vocabulary of royal sonship (see ch. 5, "David and Rule"): "You are my Son, whom I love; with you I am well pleased" (Matt. 3:13–17; Mark 1:9–11; Luke 3:21–22; John 1:32–34). David's anointing foreshadows the anointing of his descendant who will function as the perfect royal figure for Israel and bring God's rule to the ends of the earth.

For Christian readers, the role of the Spirit in the Old Testament needs to be carefully delineated, and to do this a closer look at the book of Numbers is in order. Numbers 11 relates the story of God's provision of a broader leadership corps to assist Moses in guiding the people of Israel. Here Moses was instructed to bring seventy of Israel's elders to God, who would then "take of the Spirit that is on you and put the Spirit on them" so that they might "carry the burden of the people" (Num. 11:17). Moses followed God's instructions, and the Spirit rested on the seventy elders (Num. 11:25). However, two elders who had remained in the camp were also endowed with the Spirit, and Joshua alerted Moses to this phenomenon with the concern that it should be stopped. But Moses responded: "Are you jealous for my sake? I wish that all the LORD's people were prophets and that the LORD would put his Spirit on them!" (Num 11:29). This is an important statement on the role of the Spirit at this juncture in the history of redemption and revelation. Moses' wish would be turned into prophetic hope by Joel (Joel 2:28–32) and ultimately into communal reality for the early church (Acts 2), but at the time of David God's Spirit was restricted to covenant leadership figures, setting them apart for divine service to the community.

Thus, although in one sense Christ's anointing is unique in the history of redemption, because of his anointing and subsequent request of the Father his followers can enjoy this anointing (Acts 1:4–5). This truth is presented clearly in the gospel of John where the gospel writer links the initial experience of Jesus with that of his followers:

> Then John gave this testimony: "I saw the Spirit come down from heaven as a dove and remain on him. I would not have known him, except that the one who sent me to baptize with water told me, 'The man on whom you see the Spirit come down and remain is he who will baptize with the Holy Spirit.' I have seen and I testify that this is the Son of God." (John 1:32–34)

Jesus, upon whom the Spirit has rested, is the one who will "baptize with the Holy Spirit."

This is explained more carefully in the body of teaching on the Spirit in John 14–16, and in particular in 14:16–17 when Jesus says: "And I will ask the Father, and he will give you another Counselor to be with you forever—the Spirit of truth. The world cannot accept him, because it neither sees him nor knows him. But you know him, for he lives with you and will be in you." Jesus promises to send the Spirit to his disciples. This Spirit he explains they have known because "he lives with you and will be in you." What he means here is that the Spirit has been living "with you" through Jesus, who was endowed with the Spirit at his baptism. However, he will soon be "in you," referring to Jesus' promise to send the Spirit and fulfill John's prophecy that this Jesus would "baptize with the Holy Spirit."

The anointing of David thus has implications for us as Christians for it means that as the Spirit that was upon covenant leader Moses was distributed to the seventy elders, so the Spirit that was upon covenant leader Jesus is distributed to the church, empowering us to fulfill our task as vice-regents on earth. As a messianic community we are anointed by our Messiah to fulfill his mission on earth.

FOR FURTHER REFLECTION

1. The writer of Samuel uses a narrative technique called contrast characterization to emphasize certain characters over others. To accomplish this a key character is introduced at the outset, but ultimately is eclipsed by another character who emerges out of nowhere. The first character ultimately becomes the dark foil against which we see the brilliance of the second character. Two sets of these can be discerned in the books of Samuel: one set in 1 Samuel 1–7 and the other in 1 Samuel 8–31. Can you name them? Try to discern in each case what the negative character accentuates in the positive character.

2. Although David's calling to leadership is in some ways different from that of those called to vocational ministry today, it does resonate with some of the key phases necessary for calling today. The Puritans of old often spoke of both an internal and an external calling to ministry. The internal calling was that deep sense at the core of our being of God's calling in our lives, whether that is the quiet whisper of the Spirit or the unquenchable passion to pursue a life of leadership in the church. The external calling was the gifting for public ministry, affirmed through the practice of ministry among the people of God. Such principles I think are relevant for the discernment of all vocations, since all vocations pursued by Christians are to be sanctified by God. This internal/external calling of the

Puritans echoes the private/public dimensions of the election of David to royal office in the books of Samuel. Some who are reading this book and seeking God's wisdom for their future vocation should revisit the steps of David's election and ask for confirmation from God of both internal/external, private/public dimensions of calling.

3. We learn in 1 Samuel 16 that David's anointing signified his election by God and his empowerment by the Spirit. Reflect afresh on the destination of the letter of 1 Peter: "To God's elect, strangers in the world . . . who have been chosen of God the Father, through the sanctifying work of the Spirit, for obedience to Jesus Christ and sprinkling by his blood" (1 Peter 1:1–2). How does this truth impact you in your daily walk with God?

4

DAVID AND COVENANT

Second Samuel 7 is the most helpful starting point for understanding the covenant that God established with David and his house.[1] The interchange in this chapter, however, is precipitated by another core theme of the Davidic tradition, that is, David's passion for the temple (see ch. 10, "David and Temple").

For the author of the book of Samuel, 2 Samuel 7:1 marks the end of the first phase of David's kingship, a phase marked by the creation of a royal court in his capital city ("the king was settled in his palace") and the subjugation of his enemies ("the LORD had given him rest from all enemies around him"). David, who had lived for so long in temporary quarters on the run from Saul, now realized the contrast between his fixed status in a royal palace and the enduring transitory condition of the dwelling place of God in a tabernacle legislated during the wilderness experience.

At first Nathan expressed his approval in the unspoken desires of David. But during the night the prophet received a word from the Lord for the king. In this word God questioned David's assumption that he should build a house for the Lord (7:5), reminding David that He had never used nor requested a house prior to this point in the history of Israel. God turned the tables on David who, sitting in his own completed "house" (*bayit*, palace), wanted to build a "house" (*bayit*, temple) for God. Instead, the Lord declared that he would establish a "house" (*bayit*, dynasty) for David and that the next member of that dynasty would build a "house" (*bayit*, temple) for God.

This is not the first time a promise of dynasty is mentioned in the book of Samuel. Back in 1 Samuel 13:13–14, in Samuel's first rebuke of Saul, we hear: "You have not kept the command the LORD your God gave you; if you had, he would have established your kingdom over Israel for all time. But now your kingdom will not endure; the LORD has sought out a man after his own heart and appointed him leader of his people, because you have not kept the LORD's command."

It appears that David now has reached a critical juncture in the steps toward dynasty which Saul never attained, one in which God would extend the promise of dynasty and enter into covenant relationship with David and his descendants.

COVENANT

"Covenant" is the usual translation of the Hebrew word *berith*, a term that is used on countless occasions in the Old Testament to signify a binding agreement between two parties. A *berith* may be oral or written, but in either case it provides structure to a relationship. The term is used to speak of agreements that are struck between two humans (Gen. 14:13; 31:44–55; Josh. 9:15–20) or between a human and God. It is the latter that is the focus of our attention at the moment, although as we will see in this study of David, such human-divine covenants have significant implications for the covenant relationships between human beings.

While many describe the relationship between God and humanity at creation in covenantal terms, the first divine-human covenant that employs the Hebrew technical term for covenant (*berith*) is the one established between God and Noah (Gen. 9). This covenant with all humanity after the Fall through Noah is followed by a series of covenants that are focused on the redemptive family that comes from Abraham. The covenant with Abraham is the first of these covenants (see Gen. 15 and 17), followed by the Sinai (Ex. 19-20), Priestly (Num. 25; cf. Mal. 2:1-9), and Royal (2 Sam. 7) covenants. These various covenants are not in competition with one another. Rather, they are subsumed within one another, the Sinai filling out the stipulations of the relationship that was established with the nation through Abraham (Neh. 9:7-14). In the same way, the Priestly and Royal covenants are subsumed within the Abraham-Sinai covenants. Both the Priestly and Royal lines are raised up to bring the Abrahamic promises to fruition and will be guided by and will guide the people in the ways of Torah.

GOD'S COVENANT WITH DAVID

As is typical of covenant forms in the Old Testament and actually throughout the ancient Near East, God's speech began with a review of the past relationship between himself and his covenant partner, highlighting his election of David from obscurity and his protection of David before all his enemies (2 Sam. 7:8–9a). The Lord then listed the future benefits of this covenant relationship, or better, his promises to David, which included royal fame for David, a secure kingdom for Israel and David, and an enduring dynasty for David (7:9b–16). The human responsibilities in this covenant relationship were not stressed as strongly as in other covenants such as Sinai, but were implied in the allusions to future building of the temple and future discipline of wayward members of the line (7:13–15). However, the emphasis throughout was on the eternal and immutable character of this covenant (7:16).[2]

God's speech was delivered to David through his court prophet Nathan (7:4, 17), but such promises demand a response and so David entered the presence of God, presumably the tent where the ark had been placed in 6:17. His initial response was cast in the vocabulary of humility with the self-effacing questions: "Who am I . . . What is my family . . . What more can David say to you?" His speech in 7:18–19 responded directly to God's speech to him, noting God's grace not only to "have brought me this far" (past; cf. 7:8–9a) but also to speak "about the future of the house of your servant" (future; cf. 7:9b–16). David was unwilling to highlight anything in his own behavior that would be deserving of this grace, concentrating instead on God's "word" and "will" (7:20–21). He focused then upon the greatness of God, unrivaled among the gods of the earth (7:22), and the grace of God to Israel, unrivaled among the nations of the earth (7:23–24). Only then did David respond to God's promise to establish his dynasty forever while keeping the focus on God and his people (7:25–26). David's response highlighted an important aspect of the Davidic covenant. It was ultimately not a covenant about David and his dynasty, but rather was a covenant with David for the glory of God and the sake of Israel as a nation. This promise to Israel was at the heart of God's speech to David in 7:10–11, and reemerged in David's response to God in 7:23–26. David's dynasty was to find identity and significance not in its own right, but rather in its key mediatorial relationship between God and his people, a role highlighted initially in the promised commission to build a temple for the people.

PSALM 132

It is clear that the emphasis in the account of 2 Samuel 7 was on the divine side of the covenant relationship. No reason was given in the account for the Lord's bestowal of an enduring dynasty for David. For this one must look to other passages like Psalm 132.

Among the Songs of Ascent, which were most likely used to accompany pilgrims on the ascent to Jerusalem for the feasts, Psalm 132 clearly is concerned with the fortunes of the house of David. Its opening cry ("O LORD, remember David and all the hardships he endured") suggested a period when David had undergone extreme suffering inflicted by another person.[3] Events like the revolts of Absalom or Sheba during the reign of David come immediately to mind, although the focus on the future of the Davidic house may suggest the reign of a later king or even the nightmare after the fall of Jerusalem in 587 BC. Verses 2 and 11 in Psalm 132 both begin with the same language: "X swore an oath to Y," dividing the psalm into two basic sections, the first (132:2–10) focused on David's oath to the Lord and the second (132:11–18) on the Lord's oath to David.[4] Both sections use similar language in their main body, that is, language connected to the ark in Zion (dwelling, resting place). Both sections end with a focus on David as the anointed one (132:10, 17). In each case the swearing of the oath is followed by a series of first person declarations from the covenant partner ("I will . . . "), outlining the individual's commitment to the covenant relationship. God's covenant oath in 132:11–18 is closely allied with what was already discovered in 2 Samuel 7.[5] He promises to keep David's descendants on the throne of Israel as long as they keep the Lord's covenant and declares his choice of Zion as the place of his dwelling and his commitment to bless her with provisions, salvation, and joy.

A new emphasis in Psalm 132, however, is that the divine oath is preceded by an oath declared by David which is directly related to his passion to find a dwelling place for the Lord expressed in his efforts to bring the ark from Kiriath Jearim to Jerusalem. This confirms that the Davidic covenant, which establishes an enduring dynasty for

David, is directly related to the concern expressed in the opening section of 2 Samuel 7: the creation of a permanent dwelling place for the Lord in Zion. Psalm 132, therefore, intertwines the destiny of the temple with that of the royal house in Zion, a theme that we will take up in more detail later (see ch. 10, "David and Temple").

COVENANT DISCIPLINE

While the emphasis in the Davidic covenant is clearly on God's grace and favor expressed to David and his line, one cannot ignore that with great privilege came heightened responsibility. God's promise is secure as he speaks of David's progeny: "I will be his father, and he will be my son" (2 Sam. 7:14a). However, in the very next line, without any sense of contradiction, God warns: "When he does wrong, I will punish him with a rod wielded by human beings, with floggings inflicted by human hands" (7:14b TNIV), followed immediately by the careful reminder: "But my love will never be taken away from him, as I took it away from Saul, whom I removed from before you" (7:15). By this God declares that David's progeny has the secure status of child with God as parent, but that this does not preclude discipline of those in that line who go astray. The story that enfolds in the books of Kings reveals that God indeed does follow through on both this promise and this warning. Although continuing to bless and preserve the royal dynasty because of his covenant with David, he is not averse to disciplining even David's favored son, Solomon.

IMPLICATIONS

As we mentioned in the opening chapter, the language of the Davidic covenant provides the key link between Jesus and David. In the New Testament it is the language of "sonship" as found in 2 Samuel 7:14 and Psalm 2:7 that identifies Jesus as Messiah (Matt. 3:17; Luke 3:22; Acts 13:33; Heb. 1:5; 5:5; 2 Peter 1:17).

Acts 13:33–34 reveals that the resurrection of Jesus was the ultimate fulfillment of the "holy and sure blessings promised to David" (Isa. 55:3), the details of which are provided in the covenant-making account of 2 Samuel 7. This same concept is expressed in Acts 2:25–32: "God had promised him on oath that he would place one of his descendants on his throne." Christ's resurrection thus is closely related to his enthronement at the right hand of God, vice-regent forever over the earth. Jesus unites human and divine kingship in one individual.

So accustomed are we to this message of the fulfillment of the Davidic promises in Jesus that it is easy to take it for granted and in the process lose the wonder of its truth. The early church was filled with worship toward their redemptive God who had not only made promises to his people, but accomplished them in the fullness of time. Through the darkness of the exile and under the watchful eye of empires, the community of God had longed for God to bring a royal Messiah to rescue them from their oppression. And it was in Jesus that these promises were fulfilled.

Such a witness demands our worship of the God of covenant who fulfills his promises. But it also strengthens our faith to trust God to fulfill the covenant promises at the heart of his relationship with us. This theme of covenant reinforces the fact that God is a God of relationship who invites his people into relationship guided by principles. David's passionate pursuit of relationship with God is without equal in the Old Testament, but such pursuit was shaped and guided by the covenant that is enunciated in 2 Samuel 7 and described in Psalm 132. Such passages are important reminders to those of us who now not only enjoy the blessings of the Davidic covenant, but also assume its responsibilities as the messianic community, that our gracious God has high expectations for us and will indeed discipline us as his children, just as he did the Davidic dynasty of old. Such discipline, however, is not a sign of rejection, but rather of love, and is accompanied by the promise that "my love will never be taken away from him" (2 Sam. 7:15).

Our response should be shaped by David's reply to God's covenant overtures. We should be humbled by God's offer of gracious election and blessing. We should also see the ultimate purpose of this election and blessing as the glory of God as David prayed so long ago: "And now, LORD God, keep forever the promise you have made concerning your servant and his house. Do as you promised, so that your name will be great forever. Then people will say, 'The LORD Almighty is God over Israel!'"(2 Sam. 7:25–26 TNIV).

FOR FURTHER REFLECTION

1. What are some of the covenants (whether formal or informal) that you have made in your life on the human level: whether for employment, education, church attendance, marriage, friendship? What were the core values of each of these and how were you kept accountable to these covenants?
2. Reflect on your covenant relationship with God. As noted above, ancient covenant ceremonies often began with a review of the history of the relationship between the two covenant partners, often identifying the ways in which each party has responded to the other in the past until this moment. Why not take some time now to reflect on what God would say to you about your past relationship with him and his act of grace toward you. Rehearse the core

promises that God has made to you as his child and also the core warnings. As David responded to God in prayer after God rehearsed these promises and warnings, so you can take this opportunity to write a prayer of response to God.

5

DAVID AND RULE

T he story is told in Canada of the 1939 visit of the king and queen of England to Montreal, Quebec. They were met at the airport by Montreal's three-hundred-pound Mayor Camillien Houde in an open limousine. To understand Houde's personality better it is insightful to know that he would later spend much of the Second World War in jail over his "conscientious objection" to Quebec men serving in the Canadian army. Of course, after his release he would be reelected by a large majority as mayor. The limousine carrying Houde and the queen (Queen Elizabeth's mother) rolled down Sherbrooke in the heart of royalist Montreal as all the Anglophones cheered and waved their Union Jacks. Houde leaned over to the queen and remarked: "You know, sum of diss is for you!"

The debate over kingship in Israel in our initial chapter reveals how important it was that the royal house know its proper place within the theopolitical structure of the nation. As we will see in this chapter, David's rule had no legitimacy apart from the rule of God. This foundational concept could not help but have an impact on how David approached kingship in relationship to God, but also how David treated kingship prior to his enthronement over the nation.

Enthronement

As we discussed earlier (ch. 1, "David and Biblical Theology"), the royal figure in Israel was not to consider himself the exclusive occupant on the throne. Rather the king reigned as vice-regent, exercising God's rule in Israel and ultimately throughout the entire earth. The establishment of a royal figure on his throne in Israel involved some prescribed steps: anointing with oil, empowerment by the Spirit, accomplishment of a great feat, and recognition by the nation. Evidence for the final element, the public recognition of the king, can be culled from the royal accounts of Samuel and Kings. In the case of Saul (1 Sam. 11:14–15), all the people gathered together at Gilgal and in a ceremony confirmed Saul as king in the presence of the Lord, sacrificing fellowship offerings before the Lord and celebrating his ascension to the throne. In David's case, the elders of Israel assembled at Hebron to make covenant with David before the Lord (2 Sam. 5:1–5).

In 2 Samuel 15:10–12 Absalom's enthronement is signaled by the blowing of trumpets, the announcement that Absalom is king in Hebron, the assembling of people and leaders (two hundred men from Jerusalem and the all-important Ahithophel, David's counselor), and the offering of sacrifice. At the end of David's rule, descriptions of two installations are provided as two sons of David vie for the throne. In his enthronement (1 Kings 1:5, 24–27), Adonijah arranges for chariots and horses with fifty men to run ahead of him, goes to a special place ("the Stone of Zoheleth near En Rogel"), performs great sacrifices, invites key leaders (the king's sons, commanders of the army, Abiathar the priest), feasts, and has them declare, "Long live King Adonijah!" These events signal to the people that Adonijah has become king (1 Kings 1:11, 13, 18, 24). After Adonijah's illegitimate ceremony, David sketches the ceremony that will be carried out for Solomon (1 Kings 1:32–48). Key leaders and soldiers (Zadok, Nathan, Benaiah, Kerethites, Pelethites) would place Solomon on David's mule and escort him down to the Gihon. The priest and prophet would anoint Solomon king over Israel with the horn of oil from the sacred tent. A trumpet would be blown, and all the people would shout "Long live King Solomon," play flutes, and rejoice greatly. Solomon then would sit on David's royal throne where the officials would congratulate the new king.

There is an expectation of a ceremony after the death of Solomon, and so his son Rehoboam travels to Shechem where all Israel had gone to make him king (1 Kings 12:1). However, the ceremony does not happen due to the new king's folly.

After this point in the accounts of Judah, no details are offered for the ascension of the king to his throne, except for the enthronement of Joash in 2 Kings 11:4–14, the boy king rescued from the hands of his murderous royal grandmother Athaliah. In this account, the most detailed of all of the reports, military personnel are front and central, a fact that is not surprising considering the character of Athaliah's rule, and the temple is the setting, also not surprising because this was where Joash was hidden from Athaliah. Military leaders and their troops were brought into the temple, put under oath, given weapons, and stationed themselves around the temple and altar near the king. Jehoiada, the priest, brought out Joash to a position that is explicitly identified as "by the pillar." Once in position, Jehoiada placed the royal crown on Joash's head, presented the new king with a copy of the covenant, proclaimed him king, and anointed him. The people then responded by clapping their hands and shouting "Long live the king!" accompanied by trumpets. This was followed by a covenant ceremony between the Lord, the king, and the people before the soldiers and people escorted the king from the temple through the gate of the guards to the palace where he took his place on the royal throne. While some of these elements may be unique to this enthronement in the wake of Athaliah's rule, the phrase "as the custom was" in 11:14 suggests that at least some of the elements were typical of enthronement ceremonies.[1]

These various accounts ranging from Saul to Joash suggest that there were rituals associated with the installation of a king to the throne of Israel. These included assembling leading officials within the land (priests, prophets, elders, military commanders) as well as the general population, anointing the king with oil, blowing the trumpet, declaring "Long live the king," activities that were carried out at specially designated areas. The specific liturgy which accompanied these services is never related in these narrative accounts; however, it is very likely that traces of such a liturgy are now preserved in two psalms in the Psalter, Psalm 2 and 110. These two psalms address kings who reigned in Jerusalem (Pss. 2:6; 110:2) and provide insight into the relationship between God and his anointed one.

Psalm 2

It is not difficult to see why Psalm 2 has often been linked to ceremonies connected with the enthronement of a Davidic king in Judah. It explicitly mentions the installation of a king in Jerusalem ("on Zion") on a particular day ("today"), emphasizes the triumphant rule of this king over the nations, and contains links to the oracle of Nathan to David in 2 Samuel 7:8–16. Evidence from ancient Near Eastern texts and ceremonies has confirmed this theory, noteworthy of which are the ceremony of breaking pottery into pieces in Egyptian coronation ceremonies, references to kings as "son of God," and the practice of kissing the king's feet as a sign of homage at accession.[2]

The psalm shifts between three speakers, evidence that underlying this text is a liturgy from an installation ceremony. These shifts in speakers provide the first clues for discerning the structure of the liturgy. The first section, focusing on the declaration of rebellious kings, depicts these rulers of the nations devising a conspiracy (vv. 1–3). One can see how such plots would fit the context of transition in leadership; indeed, many of the annals in the ancient Near East confirm that during such times peoples subjugated by foreign powers would seize the opportunity for independence. The scope of the conspiracy is universal, encompassing "the nations . . . the peoples" as well as "the kings of the earth . . . the rulers." The verb "take their stand" (*yatsav*) is used to refer to marshalling troops in formation (1 Sam. 17:16; Jer. 46:4), while the verb "gather" (*yasadh*) to scheming a plot (Ps. 31:13 [Heb. 14]). These two activities contrast one another, the one publicly challenging authority, while the other secretly undermining authority. Through these two methods, the agenda of these rulers is release from the hegemony of an overlord, expressed through the imagery of "chains" and "fetters."

The focus of the conspiracy, however, is not on a single overlord, but rather on "the LORD and . . . his Anointed One." The Lord is a reference to the God of Israel, Yahweh, while the Anointed One is obviously a reference to the Davidic king (see ch. 3, "David and Anointing"). The focus of their attack binds together the Lord and his anointed king as inseparable. To attack the one is to attack the other (2:2), while to submit to one is to submit to the other (2:11–12).

The warning to these rebels, however, is left unexpressed until the final section of the psalm (vv. 10–12). Before that the liturgy builds a foundation for exposing the folly of any such rebellion. The first stage occurs in the heavenly realms where the Lord's initial response is expressed (vv. 4–6). There the heavenly king laughs and scoffs at such nonsense from these earthly kings. But his laughter is but a prelude to the wrath which strikes terror in the conspirators.

What is fascinating, however, is the content of his angry tirade. Rather than pointing to the vengeance he will inflict on any who dare rebel, the heavenly king simply announces: "I have installed my King on Zion, my holy hill" (2:6). This implies what is made clear later in the psalm (2:12): the Lord has invested his authority and power in the Davidic king who has now been installed, and the rebels' fear of the human king should be commensurate with their terror before the divine king. The Lord has firmly established his representative on earth and will work through him. This reveals God as the ultimate sovereign behind the Davidic throne, but at the same time drives home that he works through his appointed individual to bring his rule on earth.

This installation takes place "on Zion, my holy hill." This may be a reference to the entire city of Jerusalem. But in light of the fact that Joash's coronation took place in the temple courts, these terms also may refer more particularly to the temple itself which, for all intents and purposes, represented the earthly portal to the heavenly palace of the divine king.

In verses 7–9 the Davidic king recounts the decree that the Lord proclaimed to him on the day of his installation on Zion. The decree (*hoq*) mentioned here may refer to the covenant mentioned in 2 Kings 11:12 that was enacted between king, people, and God. Only a portion may be actually included in Psalm 2, the fuller form including both rights (as here) and responsibilities (cf. 2 Sam. 7). By recounting the rights in the decree at installation, the rebellious rulers of the earth will realize how intimate a connection there is between the earthly royal and heavenly king.

As in the oracle of Nathan in 2 Samuel 7:14 ("I will be his father, and he will be my son"; cf. Ps. 89:26–27), sonship is central to this proclamation: "You are my Son; today I have become your Father" (Ps. 2:7). It is true that an allusion to sonship can be found in the Sinai covenant (Deut. 1:31; 8:5). However, the close association between sonship and kingship in the ancient Near East, especially at the time of coronation, suggests that this declaration in Psalm 2 is distinct. In Egyptian thought the pharaoh was considered a son of the gods, for the god Amon had begotten him with the queen mother. In Mesopotamian thought the king was considered a "servant," installed and empowered through a statement by the gods. Although aspects of these two can be discerned in the ceremony associated with the Davidic king (Egyptian sonship, Mesopotamian installation), in contrast, sonship was not achieved through conception but rather adoption, displayed in the declaration: "You are my Son, today I have become your Father."[3]

This new status of sonship grants the Davidic king the right to ask God for the realm and authority due a prince. That realm is the "nations . . . the ends of the earth" which are now his inheritance and possession. That authority has the might of an iron scepter, an offensive weapon symbolizing the unlimited power of the Davidic king. Its effect is as devastating as if one is hitting only pottery.

It is this grant of realm and authority that now completes the careful rhetorical foundation for God's response to the conspiring kings of the earth. The Davidic king they dare threaten is none other than the inheritor of their lands who wields unlimited power over them. And so verse 10 introduces the implications of this commission for these kings. They should be wise and take the warning of God seriously. They should serve the Lord, the heavenly king, with fear and trembling, and kiss the Son, symbolic of their submission to the rule of the Lord through the Davidic king (cf. Isa. 49:23).[4] If they do not follow the wise warning, they will face the wrath of the Davidic royal, who has been commissioned to dispense the wrath and anger of the Lord (vv. 5,

12). But there is the way of wisdom. For those who take refuge in the king, there is blessing from God (Ps. 72:17b).

Psalm 2 thus reveals the intimate relationship between the rule of David and the rule of the Lord. Such a coronation liturgy was a poignant reminder of the privileged status of the house of David and a warning to any subjects of the authority that the king carried from God. However, it was also an important reminder to the new king that his rule was based not on his own authority or power, but rather on the gracious election and divine authority of the Lord. It is when the Davidic kings forgot this theological foundation that they nearly destroyed their nation and almost extinguished the dynasty of the king "after God's own heart."

Psalm 110

Like Psalm 2, Psalm 110 has also been closely associated with the installation of Davidic kings. Reference is made to a "scepter" and "Zion," and direct address from God is included. Two short quotations from God punctuate the psalm at verses 1 and 4, and each of these is followed by comments about the Lord's blessing on the king.

The first quotation from God (v. 1) assures the king of his privileged status at the right hand of God. Such a position is a place of rest for the king, for he is instructed to remain there while the Lord does battle for him. The divine warrior will bring these enemies into a place of abject submission, indicated here by the image of the feet. The second quotation from God (v. 4) assures the king of his privileged and enduring status. The Lord's oath is immutable and everlasting. The privileged status, however, now is described as "a priest . . . in the order of Melchizedek." Melchizedek is known from the Old Testament account of Abraham as the "king of Salem" who also served as "priest of God Most High." Salem is most likely associated with "Jeru-salem,"[5] the city from which the mighty scepter would extend (Ps. 110:2). The Davidic dynasty here is being associated with the ancient priest-king Melchizedek who ruled and served in Jerusalem even in the time of Abraham. This casts the Davidic dynasty into an important intermediary role on earth, a role that is evident in David's association with worship and temple (see chs. 9 and 10, "David and Temple," "David and Worship").

The descriptive promises that follow each of the quotations echo the same military theme evident in Psalm 2. The first declaration (vv. 2–3) is addressed to the human king, promising authority to extend from Zion over his enemies through an army willing and numerous. The second declaration (vv. 5–7) is addressed to the divine king, describing to God how the human king (the Lord is in small capitals; cf. v. 1) is at God's right hand and from this place will crush kings and rulers and judge nations. The final image of the lifting of the head is a sign of the victory that is assured in verse 1 (cf. Pss. 3:3; 27:6; Gen. 40:13).

As with Psalm 2, Psalm 110 highlights the privileged status of the Davidic kings. At the same time, it reminds the king that his status originates with the Lord who must work on his behalf, extending his power and rule over his enemies.

These two psalms thus highlight the designated role for the Davidic king in Israel. First of all, the king was above all representative of God's rule on earth. Yahweh and the Anointed One are equated throughout this psalm, linked as Father and Son. To attack the king is to attack Yahweh. Second, the vice-regency of the Davidic royal has a global dimension: it expects nothing less than global domination of Yahweh's rule through this royal figure. This dimension is echoed in the declaration of Psalm 72:8–11:

> He will rule from sea to sea
> and from the River to the ends of the earth.
> The desert tribes will bow before him
> and his enemies will lick the dust.

The kings of Tarshish and of distant shores
   will bring tribute to him;
the kings of Sheba and Seba
   will present him gifts.
All kings will bow down to him
   and all nations will serve him.

Third, this vice-regency is totally reliant on Yahweh. Its security is not related to the resources furnished by the human king, but rather those of the heavenly king. Fourth, this vice-regency has a priestly dimension to it, that is, this king plays a mediatorial role, mediating the presence and rule of God on earth as well as within the nation. Finally, this vice-regency has a protective dimension to it. Those who "take refuge" in this vice-regent are blessed by God.

DAVID AND OTHER HUMAN RULERS

David and Saul

As we have seen, David was to rule as vice-regent of God on earth; this meant great privilege but also the responsibility to know that his authority for rule was based upon Another, not himself. The success of Davidic kings, thus, would be directly related to the ability of the human king to live in submission to the Divine King, to eschew any notions of grasping the authority of the Lord. Such an attitude toward the throne is shown not only in David's consistent displays of submission to God by seeking the divine will, but also in David's avoidance of any appearance of grasping after the throne of his predecessor Saul.

The account of Saul is at times an excruciating annal of the demise of a leader. His tenure as empowered leader is short-lived: anointed in 1 Samuel 10, confirmed by the people in 1 Samuel 11, and rejected in 1 Samuel 13 and 15 with his successor anointed by 1 Samuel 16 even as he loses the royal spirit. Nevertheless, he continues in the office of king for forty-two years until his death in 1 Samuel 31, constantly pursuing David throughout Israel. These sixteen chapters clearly highlight David's legitimacy as king over Saul. Against the dark backdrop of Saul, the brilliance of David shines more brightly.

This is demonstrated most poignantly in the contrast between Saul and David in their grasping after power. Saul's jealousy of David is undiminished throughout the latter half of 1 Samuel. On several occasions he seeks to kill David, trying to convince his family and soldiers to eradicate his foe. The jealousy is accentuated in the account by the narrator through the repetition of the saying: "Saul has slain his thousands, and David his tens of thousands" (18:7; 21:11; 29:5). In the course of the account first Jonathan, then Saul, and finally Abner admit that David is the inevitable victor and heir to the throne (1 Sam. 23:17, Jonathan; 24:20, Saul; 2 Sam. 3:9–10, Abner). Throughout this period, however, Saul is desperate to hang on to his power, even though he knows that God has rejected him and has chosen another to assume the throne.

Saul's stance contrasts sharply with that of David. On two occasions (1 Sam. 24:1–22; 26:7–14), David has ample opportunity to kill Saul and assume the throne. In both cases his colleagues identify this as the opportunity that God had promised him (24:4; 26:8). However, in both cases he refuses, declaring that it is inappropriate to touch the Lord's anointed. At one point God had anointed Saul, and David, though also anointed and the legitimate possessor of the royal spirit and throne, was unwilling to take the office for himself. Such a gift was only for God to give.

This refusal to grasp after the throne is also evident in 2 Samuel 1 and 4. When David received word of the death of Saul and his sons on Mount Gilboa, he put to death the one who dared kill the Lord's anointed. Similarly, when David received news of the death of Ish-bosheth, the son of Saul who laid claim to the throne after the death of his father, rather than rewarding the brothers who executed him, he ordered them killed. These many examples highlight David's refusal to take the throne of Israel before God had given it to him. This reticence to grasp after the throne from other human claimants reveals an important character value within David that qualified him to rule under God in Israel.

David and Absalom

David's lack of grasping after the throne and entrusting his rule into the hands of God are also evident during his own reign. Absalom's murder of his brother Amnon for raping his sister Tamar was the first sign that David's kingdom was in trouble (2 Sam. 13). Absalom fled to safety with the king of Geshur where he remained for three years (2 Sam. 13:37–39), but ultimately returned to the city through the mediation of Joab (2 Sam. 14). This return, however, would spell disaster for David and his kingdom, for Absalom conspired to have himself proclaimed king in Hebron. David realizes he has lost his power base among the people and so quickly leaves Jerusalem. His words to Zadok, his priest, as he sends the ark back to the city emphasize his implicit trust in God for his rule: "If I find favor in the LORD's eyes, he will bring me back and let me see it and his dwelling place again. But if he says, 'I am not pleased with you,' then I am ready; let him do to me whatever seems good to him" (2 Sam. 15:25–26). His humiliation before God is emphasized in the depiction of his ascent of the Mount of Olives: "But David continued up the Mount of Olives, weeping as he went; his head was covered and he was barefoot. All the people with him covered their heads too and were weeping as they went up" (2 Sam. 15:30).

David's concern for Absalom throughout the civil war that follows and ultimately his mourning over the death of his son parallel his concern for Saul before his reign. Again, David is depicted as one whose grasp on power was entrusted into the hands of the God who appointed him as vice-regent over Israel and the nations.

IMPLICATIONS

One of the hallmarks of Jesus Christ's teaching is unquestionably the kingdom of God. He proclaimed the inauguration of the rule of God on earth, something made clear in the prayer he taught his disciples to pray: "Your kingdom come, your will be done, on earth as it is in heaven" (Matt. 6:10). The realization of this kingdom, however, was to be accomplished through unique methods. The disciples are expecting the renewal of the Davidic kingdom (Acts 1), but divine methodology appears to be different. It would not be through the typical methods of might and power, but rather through one who would humbly suffer and bring the victory of God on earth.

Our consideration of David and his relationship to power has illuminated a similar value: humility. Key to the success of David and the Davidic line was a lack of grasping after power and rule, exemplified in the relationship between David as vice-regent and God as king of Israel or in the relationship between David and Saul. In both cases the Davidic royal was called to know his place and to await God's lead. No Davidide exemplified this greater than Jesus. The ancient Christian hymn now found in Philippians 2:6–11 offers us a vision of the self-humiliation of Jesus, even to the point of the cross.

Who, being in very nature God,
did not consider equality with God something to
be grasped,

but made himself nothing,
    taking the very nature of a servant,
    being made in human likeness.
And being found in appearance as a man,
    he humbled himself
    and became obedient to death—even death on a
        cross!
Therefore God exalted him to the highest place
    and gave him the name that is above every
        name,
that at the name of Jesus every knee should bow,
    in heaven and earth and under the earth,
and every tongue confess that Jesus Christ is Lord,
    to the glory of God the Father.

The theme of this hymn is evident in the earliest sermon of the church (Acts 2:29–36). Preaching to that Pentecost crowd in Jerusalem, the apostle Peter identifies the resurrection and ascension of Christ as evidence of the lordship of Christ over the nations. After citing Psalm 110:1, Peter declares: "Therefore, let all Israel be assured of this: God has made this Jesus, whom you crucified, both Lord and Christ" (Acts 2:36).

It is very clear that the humiliation of Christ ultimately led to his exaltation and was to lead subsequently to the submission of the nations. This ultimate global impact was expected by Christ and declared in one of his key postresurrection appearances. In Matthew 28:18–20 he declares: "All authority in heaven and on earth has been given to me. Therefore go and make disciples of all nations, baptizing them in the name of the Father and of the Son and of the Holy Spirit, and teaching them to obey everything I have commanded you. And surely I am with you always, to the very end of the age." This passage makes it clear that ultimately it is through his people that Christ will extend his global rule as he sends them forth to make disciples of all nations. This means that God's commission to the church is nothing less than the extension of the Davidic commission of old. As those now indwelled by the Davidic Messiah who suffered and rose again from the dead, so now we are called to declare his rule to "all nations," in word and deed. Such declaration, however, must honor the character of the one who suffered and was exalted, that is, it must be accomplished in humility and may even require suffering for the sake of the kingdom. There is no room for triumphal arrogance in the economy of God's kingdom work.

FOR FURTHER REFLECTION

1. Identify signs of God's kingdom breaking into your life, community, and/or church. Celebrate these signs where God's kingdom has come and his will is being done on earth as it is in heaven.
2. Conversely, identify areas where God's kingdom needs to break into your life, community, and/or church. Use the Lord's Prayer to pray that God's kingdom would be realized.
3. One core value of kingdom living and practice which we have identified in this chapter is that of humility and suffering. Identify the ways in which you or your faith community have displayed inappropriate grasping after power or inappropriate arrogance in relationships. Express to God your desire to more fully trust in him, his timing and purposes, and your desire to denounce grasping and pride.

6

DAVID AND FAITH

First Samuel 17 is a vital passage in the flow of the book of Samuel. Looking to the previous chapters of this book, note that David's great feat in killing Goliath and bringing victory for Israel is the fourth in a series of steps in the description of his ascension to the monarchy (see ch. 3, "David and Anointing"). These steps are illustrated first in the life of Saul who is first anointed by Samuel (1 Sam. 9–10), endowed by the Spirit (1 Sam. 10), despised by the people (1 Sam. 10), and then performs a great feat (1 Sam. 11) before being affirmed by the people (1 Sam. 11). This same pattern is repeated for David: anointing (1 Sam. 16), Spirit endowment (1 Samuel 16), despising (1 Sam. 17), great feat (1 Sam. 17). Thus, 1 Samuel 17 continues the story of the ascendancy of David to the throne, but at the same time reveals a stark contrast between Saul and David.

DAVID AND GOLIATH

As the chapter opens we are ushered into a scene taking place in the Shephelah, the series of valleys that lay between the Philistine-controlled coastal plain and the

Israelite-controlled central hill country. Just one valley over, in the Sorek, another story of encounter between Philistia and Israel took place, that of Samson and Delilah, one that ended in disaster as the powerful Israelite judge would risk all due to liaisons with this Canaanite people. As long as Philistia remained entrenched on the coastal plain, Israel could never prosper, not only because they could not spread into the rich land of the Shephelah, but more importantly, because they could not gain control of the key ancient route which cut through Philistine land, the Way of the Sea with its potential for lucrative taxes on trade moving between Africa, Arabia, Asia, and Europe. It is not surprising, then, that David's great feat would involve the Philistines, the defeat of whom would enable David and his son Solomon to build a prosperous nation.

The story, however, begins without David in the scene. Saul and his army had moved into the Shephelah to encounter the Philistines, occupying a hill opposite the Philistine army in the valley of Elah. It is not until verse 12 that we hear anything about David, who is "back at the farm" tending his father's sheep while his three brothers were on the front lines, having joined Saul's army to confront the Philistine threat. Instead we are given a detailed description of the great Philistine champion, Goliath (17:4–7), and then a dramatic presentation of his taunt (17:8–10). The key to this section of the story is found in verse 11 as we are told that "Saul and all the Israelites were dismayed and terrified." Saul, the king after Israel's heart, the king whose physical stature qualified him to lead Israel into battles, was cowering before this mighty warrior. And with that admission ringing in our ears we are introduced to David.

The narrator hardly presents his character in grandiloquent terms, emphasizing that David's older brothers were in battle and that David was the youngest of eight sons, qualified only to tend the sheep back at the family farm (17:12–15). Flashing back to the scene in the valley, the narrator does not let us forget the severity of the situation, as the tension builds for forty days with the Philistine taunting Israel every morning and evening (17:16). It is now that David is invited into the scene as his father Jesse sends supplies to his brothers in the army camp along with a bribe for the commander of their unit to keep his precious eldest sons safe (17:17–19). It is this action that stresses the insignificance of David to the nation at this point, at least in the minds of all involved. It is his older brothers who are capable of mighty feats, battling alongside their king Saul. David only serves as an agent to supply their needs.

David enters the scene just as Goliath delivers another of his tirades. The words of the soldiers in verse 25 show the desperation of King Saul who is offering the world to anyone who could defeat the mighty champion. David is intrigued by the scene and sizes it up immediately (vv. 26–27). He notes the disgrace that has come upon Israel in their inability to meet the threat of Goliath. He also articulates the true character of the army of his people, that is, they are the "armies of the living God."

David's voice, however, is soon challenged as his brother enters the scene. Any thoughts of David's greatness, displayed in his wise words, dissipate as Eliab, his oldest brother, turns on him in anger. This exchange between oldest and youngest, between soldier and shepherd, between man and boy, is preserved for us in order to stress the insignificance of David in military terms. He is no mighty warrior but a boy with little to offer in terms of military prowess. And yet he is ushered into the presence of the desperate Saul, who takes one look at him and voices our own thoughts: "you are only a boy, and he has been a fighting man from his youth" (17:33).

Somehow, however, David's defense of his abilities convinces Saul to send him into battle. Although his commission in verse 37 is one filled with the words of faith ("the

Lord be with you"), Saul's true convictions are revealed in verses 37–38 as he attempts unsuccessfully to dress David in his battle armor. This is the first sign that David would not fight Goliath with the weapons of earthly war, but with those of faith.

And as if David had not shrunk enough in this story, after the tirade of Eliab and the evaluation by Saul, Goliath has the final word, despising David as merely a "stick" fit only for a "dog." It is at this moment that David defines his kingship as he contrasts two ways of waging war. For the Philistine (and the Israelites cowering before him), war was waged "with sword and spear and javelin," but for David war was waged "in the name of the LORD Almighty, the God of the armies of Israel" (17:45). For David the power of the warrior and the quality of his weaponry were irrelevant to war in God's economy. The key was faith in the Lord in whose name he came to battle.

We know the rest of the story well as David defeats the great Goliath, breaking the confidence of the Philistines and propelling the Israelites to defeat their retreating enemy. But the narrator of the story does not end the story there. In a surprising move he concludes the narrative by ushering us back to a scene at an earlier point in the story. In verses 55–56 he grants us the vantage point of Saul watching the young David as he goes out to encounter Goliath and commissioning his general to investigate the boy's background. Then in verses 57–58, the general brings David to Saul for an interview. The significance of this conclusion to the David and Goliath story is that it reminds us that this story is not ultimately about David and Goliath, but rather about David and Saul. There is David standing face to face with Saul with Goliath's head in David's grasp.

In the book of Samuel, Saul fulfills Israel's concept of a leader, which is, according to 1 Samuel 8:10–20 and 12:12, a monarch who will lead them into battle. In 1 Samuel 17 we see how in the end Saul cannot fulfill this role. David, however, fulfills Yahweh's concept of a leader. He is the anointed one who does battle by faith in Yahweh who wages war on behalf of Israel. This foreshadows the eventual kingship of David in 2 Samuel 5:17–25 where he will be a king who seeks God's wisdom for battle and who relies upon Yahweh's armies for victory. This passage then points to David as the legitimate king, anointed of God, who rallies the troops by faith in God the source of victory. This stands in direct contrast to Saul whose rejection as king began the day he tried to go into battle without properly sacrificing to God with his representative. However, 1 Samuel 17 provides transition into the delay in David's kingship in Samuel, for the recognition of his kingship will be postponed until 2 Samuel. This act sets in motion the great seesaw battle for power between Saul and David which will consume the rest of the book of 1 Samuel until Saul's death in battle. We are able to see David and Saul face to face here, and the narrator makes clear that it is David who is anointed rather than Saul.

This chapter reminds us of the principle of David as a king of faith. Although a key step in the ascension to the throne was a great military feat, for David this would be accomplished through trust in Yahweh. In this David sets up the key role of Davidic kingship, not military strength, but rather faith.

INQUIRING OF THE LORD

Since the king was to be a catalyst for trust in God in battle, he must have a means for discerning the will of God, and there appear to be at least three legitimate avenues in Israel (1 Sam. 28:6): dreams, priests (1 Sam. 22:10; 23:6, 9), and prophets (1 Sam. 9:9). Such discernment is usually signaled in the Old Testament with the phrase: "to inquire [*sha'al*] of God/the LORD."

It is in this practice of inquiring of God that the clearest contrast between Saul and David can be discerned. The downfall of Saul, whose name ironically is derived from the Hebrew term for "inquire" (*sha'al* v. *Sha'ul*), is linked by the Chronicler to Saul's failure to inquire of the Lord and his error in inquiring through inappropriate channels:[1] "Saul died because he was unfaithful to the LORD; he did not keep the word of the LORD and even consulted a medium for guidance, and did not inquire of the LORD. So the LORD put him to death and turned the kingdom over to David son of Jesse" (1 Chron. 10:13–14).

This summary statement is borne out in the presentation of Saul's reign in Samuel and Chronicles where Saul never successfully inquires of God and in desperation uses the medium at Endor to access the spiritual realm (1 Sam. 14:37; 28:6–7). In contrast, David constantly inquires of God through appropriate means and receives a divine answer (1 Sam. 22:10; 23:2, 4, 9–13; 30:8; 2 Sam. 2:1; 5:19 [1 Chron. 14:10]; 5:23 [1 Chron. 14:14]), even before he is installed as king by the people. Although often the means of inquiry are not specified, on a few occasions it is stated that he did this through the priestly channel of the ephod (1 Sam. 23:9–13; 30:7–8), a reference to the linen clothing of the priests which contained the Urim (and Thummim), unspecified objects used for discernment (1 Sam. 23:6).

TRUST

Inquiring of God was an important aspect in the battle strategy of Israel, for it represented the human royal figure's submission to the divine king and reminded him of his complete reliance on the divine king for victory. These same values are in mind in the embargo against importing horses for war (Deut. 17:14–16; 2 Sam. 8:11; Ps. 20:7; Isa. 31:1), which would represent a reliance on military technology, rather than the Lord who should be Israel's divine warrior. Isaiah the prophet would remind David's descendants, Ahaz and Hezekiah, of this principle of trust in a much later stage of redemptive history as they faced the threat of superior foes (Isa. 7:1–9; 37:5–8). It is thus not great power and strength that distinguishes the messianic line, but rather humble trust.

IMPLICATIONS

It is interesting that God's greatest victory of all, the one to which those messengers of peace testify ("Your God reigns") in Isaiah 52:7, is a victory accomplished through the weakest of figures in the Old Testament. The "suffering servant" was rejected by humanity and yet through him God brought salvation to humanity (Isa. 52:13–53:12). In the New Testament we learn that this figure is Jesus, son of David, the one who is the author and perfecter of our faith (Heb. 12:2). As Davidic king, Jesus embodied the values of trust and faith to accomplish the ultimate victory over sin and the kingdom of darkness. His death on the cross accomplished salvation for his people and prompts us to proclaim the reign of our God.

As those who have entered into the Davidic line, we are called by Christ and empowered by his Spirit to walk in similar faith as we experience through the church the progressive realization of the great victory inaugurated through Christ's victory on the cross. We go forth as a community of faith, trusting God to defeat all powers arrayed against the living God and his purposes. As David of old, we do not put on armor like Saul's fit for battling on the human plane. Rather we put on armor that is composed of the spiritual qualities exemplified by David on that battlefield in the Shephelah. Key to this is clearly the "shield of faith," but along with this we are encouraged by Paul in Ephesians 6 to also take the "belt of truth," "breastplate of righteousness," "feet fitted with the readiness that comes from the gospel of peace," "helmet of salvation," and "sword of the Spirit" (Eph. 6:13–17). Key to this kind of faith in the face of our great enemy Satan is, finally, the practice of praying "in the Spirit on all occasions with all kinds of prayers and requests" (Eph 6:18). We go forth not with great resources or powerful technology, but rather as the weak in whom God's strength is perfected.

FOR FURTHER REFLECTION

1. This theme prompts us to worship the Author of our faith, Jesus, whose sacrifice was an act of faithful submission to and trust in the Lord. Take some time to express your worship to Jesus for his faith and faithfulness.

2. This chapter also prompts us to a life of greater faith. This does not mean that God cannot work through wisely appropriated methods within our culture, but there is a tendency as Christians in our modern world to look to methods before we seek the face of God and express our trust in him to bring his kingdom on earth. Identify the ways in which you have displayed the reliance of Saul and the Israelites on human methodology and tactics in order to further the kingdom, and express your desire for a deeper trust in God.

3. The Israelites were facing a formidable foe in Goliath and the Philistines. Identify a specific situation in your life or the life of your community at this moment that is clearly beyond your ability to solve or resolve. Approach God's throne of grace in prayer, expressing your absolute trust in the same Lord who acted miraculously on David's behalf.

4. Meditate on Ephesians 6:10–18, identifying the various parts of the armor of God described by the apostle Paul. What areas of your armor (an image for mature spiritual qualities in your Christian life) are the strongest? the weakest? What steps will you take to increase these qualities?

7

DAVID AND JUSTICE

bsalom launched his conspiracy against his father David
with a shrewd pattern of behavior (2 Sam. 15:1–12).
He would get up early in the morning and stand by the
side of the road leading to the city gate to intercept anyone who
was coming "with a complaint to be placed before the king for
a decision" (15:2). He would claim that although the griev-
ances were valid and proper, there was no one to hear the case.
Then to bolster his own worthiness for kingship he would
announce: "If only I were appointed judge in the land! Then
everyone who has a complaint or case could come to me and
I would see that they receive justice" (15:4 TNIV).

This passage makes it clear that a key role for the king
in ancient Israel was that of judge. Such a claim is not
unique to Israel as evidence throughout the ancient Near
East makes clear. Hammurabi, who lived several centuries
before David, called himself the "protecting king" and
declared in the epilogue of his great law code:

> I am the salvation-bearing shepherd, whose staff is
> straight, the good shadow that is spread over my city;
> on my breast I cherish the inhabitants of the land of
> Sumer and Akkad; in my shelter I have let them
> repose in peace; in my deep wisdom have I enclosed

them. That the strong might not injure the weak, in order to protect the widows and orphans . . . in order to declare justice in the land, to settle all disputes, and heal all injuries.[1]

Evidence of David's role as judge can be discerned at various points. We are told in 2 Samuel 8:15 that David's reign over all Israel was typified by "doing what was just and right." Nathan's prophetic attack on David over the Bathsheba affair appears to employ language drawn from David's court of justice, for it elicits from David a fiery legal decision: "As surely as the LORD lives, the man who did this deserves to die! He must pay for that lamb four times over, because he did such a thing and had no pity" (2 Sam. 12:5–6). This legal role is displayed clearly in 2 Samuel 14:4–20 (here see the language of 14:17, "discerning good and evil") as Joab tricks David into allowing Absalom to return to Jerusalem by using a woman seeking justice from the king. Such a role endures in the reign of Solomon, exemplified in his wise ruling between the two prostitutes, an incident that concludes with this observation: "When all Israel heard the verdict the king had given, they held the king in awe, because they saw that he had wisdom from God to administer justice" (1 Kings 3:28).

This link between justice and kingship is also evident in the prophetic witness, which consistently looked for a Davidic ruler who would reign wisely, by maintaining justice and righteousness in the nation (Isa. 9:7; 11:1–5; 16:5; 32:1; Jer. 23:5; 33:15; cf. Isa. 42:1–7; 61:1–3).[2] The standard for this justice is identified in Deuteronomy 17:18–20 as the Torah, a copy of which the king is to provide for himself so that he may read it "all the days of his life" and "follow carefully all the words of this law and these decrees," not turning "from the law to the right or to the left." As the one through whom God would exercise his cosmic rule on earth, the Davidic king was responsible to care for the vulnerable and helpless.

Such a responsibility finds its origins in the kingship of God himself. Psalm 146, which calls Israel to trust in the eternal king of creation rather than in mortal princes who cannot save, presents a list of God's just actions as an expression of his faithfulness (146:7–9):

> He upholds the cause of the oppressed
>   and gives food to the hungry.
> The LORD sets prisoners free,
>   the LORD gives sight to the blind,
> the LORD lifts up those who are bowed down,
>   the LORD loves the righteous.
> The LORD watches over the alien
>   and sustains the fatherless and the widow,
>   but he frustrates the ways of the wicked.

This list reveals that the maintenance of justice had both a positive and a negative aspect. The main focus is the positive action of upholding the cause of the oppressed, represented in actions that rectify the plight of those who are vulnerable within the society. However, there is also a negative aspect, that is, frustrating the schemes of the wicked who threaten the cause of the oppressed. It is God's attention to both uphold the cause of the oppressed and frustrate the ways of the wicked, that distinguishes the Lord as king, for verse 10 declares: "The LORD reigns forever, your God, O Zion, for all generations." The rule of God is typified by attention to justice.

PSALM 72

Since the Davidic king was vice-regent of the Lord on earth (see ch. 5, "David and Rule"), it is not surprising then that these same actions and qualities of justice are linked to the Davidic king in the narratives and poems of Israel. This is displayed most vividly in Psalm 72 which is linked in the Psalter tradition to both Solomon (Ps. 72 super-scription) and David (Ps. 72:20). This evidence suggests that it was created by David in reference to Solomon, a con-clusion supported by the reference to the "royal son" (lit., "son of the king") in verse 1.

One of the major emphases of Psalm 72 is the blessing which accompanies the rule of the Davidic king. Such blessing is articulated at two points in the psalm: verses 5–11 and verses 15–17. Both stanzas focus on the multidi-mensional character of this blessing. First, the temporal quantity of the reign is eternal, enduring as long as the sun and moon, through all generations, that is, forever (vv. 5, 17). Second, the spatial quantity of the reign is universal (vv. 8–11, 15), extending "from sea to sea" and "from the River to the ends of the earth" while embracing the "desert tribes" to the "kings of Tarshish . . . Sheba and Seba" (cf. Ex. 23:31; 1 Kings 4:21; 5:1; Mic. 7:12; Zech. 9:10; Gen. 15:18).[3] The dimensions of this dominion are summed up in verse 11: "All kings will bow down to him and all nations will serve him."

This eternal and universal reign produces unprece-dented prosperity for the Davidic king's subjects. This is described in Psalm 72 with images drawn from the natu-ral world: rain falling, showers watering (v. 6), producing in turn: grain abounding, fruit flourishing, grass thriving (v. 16). Such abundance is linked to the "righteous" in verse 7, those faithful citizens of the kingdom who enjoy "great peace/prosperity" (*rov shalom*, "prosperity will abound"). Such prosperity, however, is not limited to those in Israel, for the final lines of the poem reveal how the Davidic king will realize the promise given to Abram (Gen. 12:3), that is, the blessing of "all nations" (v. 17b).[4]

The benefits experienced by the Davidic king according to Psalm 72, therefore, include an eternal and universal reign typified by great prosperity not only for the righteous of Israel, but also for all nations. Through the Davidic king, the promise given to Abraham to bring blessing to the entire earth is to be realized.

This ideal picture of quantitative blessing and prosperity, however, is based on an important qualification. Making this all possible is the moral quality of justice that will typify the king's reign. This is why it is the "righteous" who will flourish "in his days" (v. 7); only those whose character matches the character of the king will prosper.

The just reign of the king is described very carefully in verses 2–4 and verses 12–14. Key to such a reign is the moral compass of "righteousness" and "justice" (v. 2), qualities that typify conformity to an ethical standard or norm set by God and his law. Those who are the beneficiaries of this righteous justice are most often those who could be abused most easily by society, referred to in this psalm as the afflicted (ones), (children of) the needy, and the weak (vv. 2, 4, 12, 13). The one who should fear this righteous justice is called the oppressor, who brings death, oppression, and violence (vv. 4, 13, 14).

The king is called to administer justice (v. 4, "defend"), a verb denoting the general idea of maintaining justice in the royal court. This action is broken down into two actions in the following two lines: "save" and "crush." The administration of justice will mean the positive action of saving the vulnerable within society, that is, taking initiative to rescue them from oppression and violence (see the verbs in vv. 12–14: "deliver," "help," "save," "rescue"). But it also entails the courageous negative action of crushing those who shamelessly oppress the vulnerable (v. 4). The Hebrew word translated here as "crush" (*dakha'*) is one often used to describe the oppression of the oppressor (Isa. 3:15; Pss.

94:5; 143:3; Job 22:9; Prov. 22:22), its use here highlighting the ironic reversal that only the king could accomplish.

This dual dimension of administering justice, one positive and the other negative, is strikingly similar to the dimensions of divine justice encountered in Psalm 146. In light of this, it is not then surprising that the initial and dominant request of Psalm 72 is for God to "endow the king with your justice . . . the royal son with your righteousness" (v. 1). For the king to enact God's justice will mean nothing short of an infusion of God's character of justice and righteousness. This infusion brings to mind the anointing of the king by the Spirit of God, and it is interesting that in the prophetic tradition the endowment of the Spirit is linked to the administration of justice (Isa. 11:1–5; cf. 42:1–8; 61:1–3).

Psalm 72 thus establishes the truth that the king's administration of justice, especially in relation to the vulnerable within his kingdom, is the cornerstone of the royal office and the basis for prosperous rule. This is possible only as God endows his Davidic vice-regent with his character of justice and righteousness.

IMPLICATIONS

In the gospel of Luke one of the first recorded acts of Jesus' ministry takes place in his hometown of Nazareth. He had returned from the temptation in the wilderness "in the power of the Spirit" and began to teach in the synagogues of Galilee. Reaching his hometown on the Sabbath, he stood to read from the scroll of the prophet Isaiah these words:

The Spirit of the Lord is on me,
    because he has anointed me
    to preach good news to the poor.

He has sent me to proclaim freedom for the prisoners
   and recovery of sight for the blind,
to release the oppressed,
   to proclaim the year of the Lord's favor. (Luke
      4:18–19)

With all the eyes in that synagogue fixed upon their native son, he declared: "Today this Scripture is fulfilled in your hearing." Jesus' ministry began with the declaration that he had come to inaugurate a new era, one typified by the administration of justice for the vulnerable within society.

Such a tone is apparent throughout his ministry as he lives a life among the poor and powerless of the countryside rather than the privileged and powerful of the urban elite. It is not surprising that his entrance into Jerusalem leads to his death on a cross, the shameful end of the lower caste of his society.

So also we as Christians must fulfill Christ's role as catalyst for justice within our world. The book of Acts traces the rhythms of an early Christian community for whom the care for the poor and needy was the natural outflow of a life transformed by Jesus Christ. Acts 2:44–45 describes a community willing to share their possessions, selling them when needed to give to those who had need. Acts 4:32–37 records a community which denied their claim to their possessions, selling land and property if need be to help their fellow believer, so that the writer of Acts could claim: "there were no needy persons among them." This was a community known for its care for the vulnerable, the poor as seen in Acts 2 and 4, but as Acts 6 shows, also the widows within their care. Widows, often noted in the Old Testament among the most vulnerable class of Israel, were given a daily distribution of food by the community of Jesus (1 Tim. 5:9).

Such practices are not surprising for a community that followed Jesus. Not only had he inaugurated his ministry by announcing the new age of messianic justice from Isaiah 61, but his teaching is filled with principles that echo this message. Fundamental to this message is the conviction of Christ that his followers seek first God's kingdom and righteousness, entrusting themselves into the divine care of one who would provide for all their needs (Matt. 6:25–34). Because of this he could command the rich young ruler in Matthew 19:21 to go and sell his possessions and give them to the poor. This man was to seek first God's kingdom by loosening his grip on his possessions and by giving to the poor (cf. Luke 12:22–34; 18:22).

Elsewhere in the New Testament, however, we learn that the church was as vulnerable as Israel of old to the charge of social injustice. James reminds his readers to avoid any hint of injustice by favoring the rich over the poor in their community (James 2:1–7). It is their discrimination against the poor that is the catalyst for James's call to love their neighbor as themselves and to show their faith by their deeds (James 2:8–26). Paul berates the church at Corinth for enjoying their feasts while some within the faith community remain hungry (1 Cor. 11:17–34). To be the community of the Messiah means assuming the role of catalyst of justice within the faith community but also within society as a whole.

The example of David is instructive for the messianic community today. It reminds us that care for the poor will entail the positive action of rescuing the vulnerable within our society, that is, occupying ourselves with the agenda of the poor of our community, providing food, shelter, and counsel to those whose lives are in tatters either due to their own folly or to injustice within the very fabric of our society. It also reminds us of the need for the negative action of frustrating the abusive actions of those who would dare oppress the poor and vulnerable, whether that is by confronting unjust government policy or interceding for the poor with someone whose actions have placed their lives at risk.

This positive and negative agenda will entail individual acts of compassion, but will also mean a more concerted effort to deal with larger systems of injustice that are found within our society as a whole. This means that some in the church will need to devote their lives to advocacy for the various groups of the vulnerable within our communities. This is often difficult within the Western context in which we live, for there is an underlying belief that all human beings are responsible for their own actions and thus that one's present predicament is the result of one's own irresponsibility. Additionally, there is a tendency to see such issues as the responsibility of the government agencies to which we pay our taxes. However, not only is it obvious to most that many are slipping through the cracks of these well-intentioned systems, but it is important that the church embrace fully their kingdom responsibility for the vulnerable of our society and world.

FOR FURTHER REFLECTION

1. The early church practiced caring for those who were needy within their midst. As you think about the community of faith where you worship, whom would you classify as the vulnerable within that church community? How can you as an individual or as a family reach out in practical ways to these people? In what ways can the church as a whole, either through a shift in programing or budget priorities, begin to address the needs of those within the household of faith?

2. We certainly learn the sensibilities and rhythms of social compassion in our care for those within our families and faith communities, but the vision of justice and blessing in the Old Testament was one that extended beyond the borders of the covenant

community, to the aliens in their midst and the nations beyond. As you reflect on the community that surrounds your church, what would justice and blessing look like in a practical way using the present resources of your faith community? As you reflect on your place within the global village, how can you contribute to the alleviation of acts or results of injustice in our world today?

8

DAVID AND UNITY

My fascination with the city of Jerusalem began when I was a young boy. My father had been invited to lead a trip to Israel and upon his return was loaded with stories and slides to pass the cold Canadian winter. From that moment on I desired to go to this biblical city in order to make my own pilgrimage, and the further I progressed in my education the more the desire burned. That opportunity finally came in 1993 financed by Cambridge University.

Getting from Cambridge, England, to Jerusalem, Israel, is no easy task: with terrorist threats on both ends, from the IRA to the PLO, even boarding an airplane or bus became a major undertaking. The security guards pored over my suitcases at both Heathrow and Ben Gurion, looking for bombs or guns or the like. Then it was on to a bus route from Tel Aviv to Jerusalem and then finally the mile walk to the guest home where I was staying. I have never felt so alone in my life, making my scholastic pilgrimage to Jerusalem.

The expectancy and excitement and yet apprehension and fear I felt on my journey to Jerusalem would not even begin to approach the emotions felt by the Hebrew pilgrims of old as they approached the holy city. Three times each year the Israelites were called to the holy city, Jerusalem: to make pilgrimage to the center of their spiritual life as a nation and people. But they were not alone. Besides the throngs of worshipers that would accompany them, the pilgrims were granted a wonderful gift: the Psalms.

In Hebrew they are called *shir hamma'aloth*, in English, the Psalms of Ascent, and they stretch from Psalm 120 through to Psalm 134. As you read them, they give you a sense of a journey from far off, even outside the borders of Israel, to the very heart of Hebrew worship: Zion, Jerusalem, the temple mount, and the holy of holies itself. Even after Jerusalem had been destroyed, these psalms lived on as the great hope of the Jews in exile. Spread throughout the known world, the regular recitation of these psalms offered hope of a return to the homeland.[1]

One of my recent tours of Israel was different from the typical tour. Because we wanted to be in Jerusalem on the weekend, we began our trip heading to the far north of Israel. After touring many of the sites in Jesus' ministry using the Sea of Galilee resort of Ein Gev as our base, we began the journey to the south along the great rift valley from the Sea of Galilee, along the River Jordan, to the Dead Sea. By the time we were finished touring Qumran late in the afternoon we were ready to flop in our bus for a comfortable air conditioned ride to Jerusalem, happy that we were not like the pilgrims of old on foot or donkey, because the road from Jericho to Jerusalem rises from the lowest point in Israel to one of the highest.

Our first glimpse of the ancient city came with the setting sun behind the city, creating a spectacle as the city appeared to glow in the distance, the light stone of its medieval walls, towers, and gates gleaming as crystal. The reaction in the bus was electric, students rushing to the closest window to catch their first glimpse of the famous city. Within minutes they would be standing within the gates of the city, and the excitement was evident on their faces.

Psalms 120, 121, and 122 retrace our journey on that journey. There is a sense of movement in the two initial songs of this collection. With the words "Woe to me," Psalm 120 envisions an Israelite far away in Meshech, a slave among a caravan of Arabians.[2] Psalm 121 depicts the Israelite then moving along the hill country, picking one's way toward Jerusalem and God's presence, confidently declaring: "My help comes from the LORD, the Maker of heaven and earth." Psalm 122 ushers the pilgrims into the gates of Jerusalem. As they sing on pilgrimage still far away from Jerusalem, they imagine themselves at the entrance into the city of Jerusalem, as they declare: "I rejoiced with those who said to me, 'Let us go to the house of the LORD.'"

PSALM 122

At the outset of this psalm, the tone is clearly one of joy. Going to worship God was not seen as a begrudging duty at the time of harvest, but rather the natural expression of people in joyful relationship with the Lord. Accompanying this attitude of joy was a deep sense of community: "Let us go." The core value at the outset is that of community. We go together, we journey together. This sets the tone for what will follow in this psalm: pilgrimage is a communal activity, we do not journey alone.

In our westernization of the Christian faith we have reduced our Christian experience to the individual. We have little sense in our churches of the intimate relationship between believers that typified the early church. As we read through the book of Acts we admire but do not replicate their practices. What do we do with such passages as these?

All the believers were together and had everything in common. They sold property and possessions to give to anyone who had need. Every day they continued to meet together in the temple courts. They broke bread in their homes and ate together with glad and sincere hearts, praising God and enjoying the favor of all the people. And the Lord added to their number daily those who were being saved. (Acts 2:44–47)

All the believers were one in heart and mind. No one claimed that any of their possessions was their own, but they shared everything they had. . . . There were no needy persons among them. For from time to time those who owned land or houses sold them, brought the money from the sales and put it at the apostles' feet, and it was distributed to anyone who had need. (Acts 4:32–35)

The expression of the first verse of our psalm calls us to the following declaration: "I want to be with God's people, and I am strengthened and challenged by those who journey with me to Zion."

The psalm continues as the pilgrims testify, "Our feet are standing in your gates, O Jerusalem" (v. 2). They now imagine themselves standing within the gates of Jerusalem. The joy which accompanied the invitation to journey to Jerusalem continues as the pilgrims imagine themselves entering the city itself. They pause for a moment to reflect on the scene which greets them as they stand in the gate. Their view from this vantage point is described in verses 3–5.

The phrase at the center of this section of Psalm 122 is *lehodhoth leshem YHWH*, "to give thanks to the name of the LORD" (sometimes translated as "to praise the name of the LORD"). *Lehodhoth* is Hebrew for "to give thanks" and fits the context of the festivals at which the Israelites gave to God a portion of their harvests in thanksgiving for his bountiful care for them as Creator and gracious rescue of them as Redeemer (see ch. 9, "David and Worship").

It is this corporate aspect which highlights the key issue of unity which surrounds this central phrase in verses 3–5. The initial impression of the psalmist as he stood gazing at the city from the vantage point of the gate was that "Jerusalem is built like a city that is closely compacted together" (v. 3). Now I will admit that for a boy who grew up on the wide-open prairie of Western Canada, a trip to Jerusalem was a tad intimidating. I can remember the first time I stood outside the Damascus gate in Jerusalem and watched a multitude of people streaming into the old city through the small opening in the gate. As you descend from the modern street above to the old gate, you get the feeling that you are jumping into a sea of humanity and are carried along by the current of bodies to the other side. The city of Jerusalem today dates to the medieval period, but from archaeological records this city recreates the same feel of the ancient experience of the Israelites with its narrow streets filled with bodies wreaking havoc on ALL five senses: sight, sound, taste, touch, and especially smell! In contrast to my fears, even my repulsion at times, at the closeness of humanity in Jerusalem today, the psalmist celebrates this quality of Jerusalem, for he sees this picture of God's people compacted together as God's means to receive glory to his name.

Building on the name "Jerusalem" there are two phrases on either side of the central purpose statement in verse 4 (*lehodhoth leshem YHWH*, to give thanks to the name of the LORD) which fill out this aspect of the community of God's people:

That is **where** [*sham*] the tribes go up,
    the tribes of the LORD,

To give thanks to the name [*shem*] of the LORD

    [lehodhoth leshem YHWH]

   according to the statute given to Israel,

There [*sham*] the thrones for judgment stand,

    the thrones of the house of David.

The English words "where" and "there" both represent the same underlying Hebrew word (*sham*), and both refer to Jerusalem. The word *sham* is a deliberate echo of the central focus of the praise of Israel in the central purpose statement: (*shem*, name), creating an inseparable union between the place of unity (there, Jerusalem) and the purpose of unity (the name of the LORD).

The two appearances of *sham* (where/there) fill out two facets of the community of God. First of all, *sham* (where) in verse 4 emphasizes the unity of God's people at Jerusalem from tribal diversity: for "that is where the tribes go up, the tribes of the LORD." The people of God were a diverse people, a people from many walks of life, from many tribes in different parts of the land. The story of Israel accentuates their unity as they travel together across the vast wilderness to the Promised Land, but once in the land the early years of existence are described as a period of fractured relationships for the people of God. The book of Judges tells us of tribe fighting against tribe, of a fractured nation descending into false worship and wicked practices. The ultimate expression of this comes late in the book of Judges when, in a horrendous story, men from the tribe of Benjamin brutally rape and kill a woman from another tribe, and the other tribes rise up to punish Benjamin and nearly extinguish them from Israel.

The psalmist sees a radically different picture in his day: as he enters the city of God, Jerusalem, Zion, he sees the tribes united together; he sees Danite with Benjaminite, Ephraimite with Judahite; he sees a city compacted together and a portrait of unity for the purpose of worship.

People from vastly different worlds from the far northern mountains of Galilee to the southern deserts of the Negev, from the coastal plain of the Mediterranean to the valley of the Jordan were gathered together in unity to give thanks to the name of the Lord. These two themes, unity and worship, are so intimately connected in this psalm that they can never be abstracted the one from the other. For Israel to worship meant they must be united, and their true unity could be expressed only through common worship.

We have already noted in our opening chapter that the unity of the tribes in Israel was stipulated in the foundational document of Israel, the Torah, as Moses instructed the tribes to gather at a central place of worship when they had conquered the Promised Land. It is this instruction that is alluded to in Psalm 122:4: "according to the statute given to Israel."

That is the first *sham* (where), the first facet of the theme of unity, but we find a second *sham* (there) in verse 5: "There the thrones for judgment stand, the thrones of the house of David." It is this second *sham* (there) that makes possible the first *sham* (where), that is, the unity of the tribes in worship.

As we will note (see ch. 9, "David and Worship"), the Davidic king in Israel built a capital city, ultimately not with a political agenda in mind, but rather with a worship agenda. When David became king in Israel, the tribes were disunified, they were fighting in a bitter civil war, the ten northern tribes following the family of Saul, the two southern tribes following David. During this period David set up his capital in the southern city of Hebron, far from the fighting and the northern tribes, but the book of Samuel informs us that David's army defeated Saul's, and his first move as king was to transfer his capital from Hebron in the south to the central city of Jerusalem. Once he took that city, he brought into it the ark of God, the sign of God's rule in Israel, and the tabernacle.

David and the kings who would follow him were to play a crucial role in uniting the disparate tribes together for the purpose of worship. David's foolish grandson Rehoboam would fail miserably in this role, and the northern tribes would rebuff the Davidic crown in favor of their own rival monarchy (1 Kings 12:1–24). It is not surprising that the first act of that new kingdom's sovereign, Jeroboam, was to establish two sanctuaries in northern Israel at Bethel (south) and Dan (north) to ensure his citizens did not return to Jerusalem under the authority of a Davidic king (1 Kings 12:25–33). However, when this project failed before the might of Assyria in the late eighth century B.C. due to idolatry (2 Kings 17), Davidic kings would again play a role in uniting the tribes for pure worship at Jerusalem (2 Chron. 30–31, 34–35).

IMPLICATIONS

Christ Unifies Worship

Jesus reveals his role as Davidic unifier of worship in his fascinating encounter with the unnamed Samaritan woman in John 4. At the time of Jesus the Samaritans had established their worship of the Lord on Mount Gerizim in the northern part of Israel, an act that many Jews linked to the earlier history of rival sanctuaries in the northern kingdom (cf. 2 Kings 17; Ezra 4:1–5). The tension between Samaritan and Jew on this very issue is clearly articulated by the woman in John 4:20: "our fathers worshiped on this mountain, but you Jews claim that the place where we must worship is in Jerusalem." But Jesus shocks her when he declares:

Believe me, woman, a time is coming when you will worship the Father neither on this mountain nor in

Jerusalem. You Samaritans worship what you do not know; we worship what we do know, for salvation is from the Jews. Yet a time is coming and has now come when the true worshipers will worship the Father in spirit and truth, for they are the kind of worshipers the Father seeks. God is spirit, and his worshipers must worship in spirit and in truth. (John 4:21–24)

In this short speech, Jesus transforms the earlier stipulation of unified worship at Jerusalem by speaking about a coming time when "true worshipers will worship the Father in spirit and truth." He can claim this because of his authority as Davidic Messiah (see 4:25–26). He does not define precisely the new location ("neither on this mountain nor in Jerusalem"), except to say that it is related to worshiping "in spirit and in truth." However, this speech is anticipated at two earlier points in the gospel of John where there is allusion to Jesus as the new central place of worship.

First, in John 1:14 we are told that "the Word became flesh and made his dwelling among us. We have seen his glory, the glory of the One and Only, who came from the Father, full of grace and truth." The Greek term underlying "made his dwelling" is sometimes translated "tabernacled," because the term contains the same root used for the tabernacle in the Greek translation of the Old Testament. That this was in the mind of the gospel writer is confirmed by the reference to "the glory" and "full of grace and truth," terms associated with the presence of God that ultimately would fill the tabernacle in the book of Exodus (cf. Ex. 33–34, 40).

Second, in a heated encounter with the Jews in John 2:19–22, Jesus reveals that he is about to become the replacement for the temple through his death and resurrection. As Davidic son, Jesus now declares that he is the central place of worship through whom the people of God will worship the Lord.

This principle of unity in worship is immediately driven home by Jesus to his Jewish disciples following his encounter with the Samaritan woman in John 4. Upon their return from obtaining food in the Samaritan village, the disciples are surprised to find him talking with her. As they are about to eat, many Samaritans from the village approach them, and Jesus declares to his disciples that these Samaritans are a harvest of eternal life. On that day, the gospel tells us, many of the Samaritans believed. In this account Jesus is depicted as the unifier of Israel through belief in him.

Christians and Unity

The church is a diverse community, many tribes and potentially many tribal agendas. However, God has saved us and placed us into one body together to worship him. This unifying is accomplished by the ultimate Davidic king, the Messiah, the anointed one, the one who died on the cross to unite us together as his people, who sits upon the throne of David and calls us to truly be his body, an expression, an extension of his person on earth.

As I stood atop my hotel next to the Jaffa Gate in the old city of Jerusalem a few years ago, I took my final gaze over the city of Jerusalem. It was early evening, and the sun once again as several days before was setting, casting its illuminating rays over this fascinating city, but this time my perspective was from inside the city, rather than from a distance. Two brilliant domes caught my attention: the one closer to me and to my left was the silver Church of the Holy Sepulcher, the central shrine of Christian pilgrims, built on the traditional site of Christ's burial; and in the distance the gleaming gold Dome of the Rock, the central shrine of Muslim pilgrims, built on the foundations of the Jewish temple. In the street below was an inordinate amount of people for this late hour. Gathered around in groups of thirty were young Israeli defense soldiers, men and women with machine guns over their backs listening to their squadron captains taking them on the obligatory tour of Jerusalem.

Two domes, a city divided, a city in tension, the city called "peace" (Jeru-"salem" = "shalom") was and is a city marked by strife, tension, and hatred. In contrast to the psalmist of old I stand at the gates of Jerusalem and, although I see a city compacted together, I see disunity, strife, and hatred. But far more heartbreaking for me is to stand in the gates of Jerusalem, the people of God, the body of Christ, the church, and observe the condition of the church divided over their fundamental purpose, worship. Our only hope is to return to the foot of the cross and to bow our knee in submission to the one who through the cross ascended to a throne. To drop our differences and unite together as the body of Christ. To learn to live together in unity by living in step with the Spirit of Christ who dwells within.

These shining domes are images of irony in my mind. On the one side, I see a golden dome, the traditional site of the temple of old, the destination of the Israelite pilgrims of old in the city of God, while on the other, a silver dome, the traditional site of the burial of Christ, the Davidic king rejected by his own people as he came to unite them in worship to God. And yet in the most unique twist of history: Christ's death became the pathway to central worship, the pathway to know God and the foundation for the creation of a community who would worship God in spirit and truth.

Someday if you have the opportunity to go to Jerusalem and visit the Church of the Holy Sepulcher, you will see above the main entrance an old wooden ladder. If your tour guide is not in a hurry, he or she will tell you that this ladder is the result of a deep disagreement between the various Christian religious groups which care for the Church of the Holy Sepulcher: the Catholics, Orthodox, Armenians, and others. Squabbling over who was in charge of which area of the church and thus who would have the right to clean any particular area, two groups became upset over who had the right to wash some windows over the main entrance. The ladder remains behind as an enduring symbol of this disagreement, for the two groups did not find resolution.

What a sad commentary on the state of the church! Though Christ came to bring unity in worship to God and died upon a cross to open the way to God in exclusive worship through him, his followers blaspheme his sacrificial act and the name of God by squabbling over a ladder.

In a recent survey of Canadians by a sociologist, a consistent trend was observed among people: they like Jesus, they just don't like the church. This is a sad commentary on the state of Christ's body, the church, which according to the New Testament witness was to become the ultimate temple of God's presence on earth (1 Cor. 6:19). What often turns people off from the church is the relational disunity that reeks of hypocrisy, but what attracts them is the fragrance of brothers and sisters who have learned to live with one another and love each other deeply from the heart.

And so my prayer is that of the psalmist who prays for the peace and prosperity of Jerusalem in Psalm 122:6–9:

> "May those who love you be secure.
> May there be peace within your walls
>   and security within your citadels."
> For the sake of my brothers and friends,
>   I will say, "Peace be within you."
> For the sake of the house of the LORD our God,
>   I will seek your prosperity.

Such a prayer reminds us not only to pray for the peace of Jerusalem, the New Jerusalem, the church of Christ, but also to practice such peace as we worship our unifying Davidic king.

FOR FURTHER REFLECTION

1. This chapter has highlighted the key role of the royal house in uniting the people of God together in worship. This should prompt our thankfulness for the role that Jesus played as uniting messianic figure, not just through his leadership, but most importantly through his sacrifice on the cross. In and through Jesus' death and resurrection we enjoy the privilege of access to God. Take a moment to thank God for this indescribable gift.

2. This chapter, however, also reminds us of the high premium placed on unity in the ancient kingdom of David and in the early church. It is interesting that today a common flashpoint for disunity is worship, interesting in light of the intertwining of these two themes which we have seen in this chapter. Take a moment to reflect on any issues (possibly worship) that have divided your community of faith. Pray for the healing of relationships in light of our common faith in Jesus Christ who died to secure unity for all ages.

3. Psalm 122 is placed among the Psalms of Ascent which remind us that we are on a journey to God's presence. For the ancient Israelites that was to Jerusalem, but for Christians today that is God's ultimate presence in the heavenly Jerusalem. Psalm 84 reminds us of the passion to be in God's presence and highlights the commitment of God to strengthen those whose hearts are

set on pilgrimage. Psalm 121 reminds us that this journey is possible only because of God's protection and care. Read these two psalms and use them as catalysts for prayer.

4. Among the Psalms of Ascent, Psalm 122 accentuates the key role that community plays in the journey to Zion. Reflect on those who have been catalysts for your journey of faith, who have encouraged you with words similar to those of Psalm 122:1: "Let us go to the house of the LORD." Thank God for these people by name and/or ask God to bring these kinds of companions alongside you for a journey that involves risk and always entails faith.

9

DAVID AND WORSHIP

One of David's first initiatives, once he had ascended the throne of Israel and had vanquished his internal enemies (2 Sam. 2–4), was to capture Jerusalem. Sociologically and politically this was an important move. Jerusalem was located at the southern edge of the Benjaminite plateau, that section of Israel which not only accommodated the insignificant tribe of Benjamin, but also separated the powerful northern Joseph tribe of Ephraim from its powerful southern counterpart Judah. It is uncertain whether Jerusalem had been sacked in the original conquest of the land (Josh. 15:8; 18:16); however, after the death of Joshua the tribe of Judah had taken Jerusalem and burned it with fire (Judg. 1:8). Nevertheless, it appears that the inhabitants soon returned and the weaker Benjaminites were unable to dislodge them (Judg. 1:21).

David's capital during the seven years he ruled only the southern tribe of Judah was in Hebron, deep within the territory of Judah. The shift to Jerusalem allowed him to remain within his power base of Judah while keeping a close eye on the northern tribes which had supported the house of Saul in the civil war that brought David to power.

Furthermore, the city itself did not have previous affiliation with any of the tribes and so was a neutral location.

Whatever sociological and political agenda can be discerned in David's capture of Jerusalem, there is an unmistakable theological dimension to this action. By defeating his key external enemies the Philistines (2 Sam. 5), David was freed to focus attention on his priorities and the first of these was to bring the ark of God into Jerusalem, the first of several initiatives which would mark Jerusalem as the theological center of Israel.

DAVID BRINGS THE ARK INTO JERUSALEM

Shiloh had served as the central sanctuary of Israel in the period prior to Saul's reign (1 Sam. 4:4), and the ark remained there until it was lost to the Philistines in the great defeat described in 1 Samuel 4. The Philistines soon discovered the disadvantage of possessing this ark (it had caused a plague) and so after seven months desperately returned it to the Israelites (1 Sam. 5–6). The initial destination was Beth Shemesh, to which the Philistines sent the ark on a "new cart" pulled by cows (1 Sam. 6:7–8), but the inhabitants of Beth Shemesh were judged for foolishly looking into the ark and so relayed it on to the house of Abinadab in the city of Kiriath Jearim (1 Sam. 7). Abinadab's son Eleazar cared for the ark until David set out to bring it to Jerusalem.

The purpose of this transfer is evident in the fact that David joined other Israelites in "celebrating with all their might before the Lord, with songs and with harps, lyres, tambourines, sistrums and cymbals" (2 Sam. 6:5). The transfer of the ark to Jerusalem was to place God at the center of their national life, making Jerusalem the central site of worship of the Lord. But the transfer of the ark to Jerusalem would be no easy task. Following the lead of the

Philistines, David placed the ark on a "new cart," guided by two other sons of Abinadab, Uzzah and Ahio. When the oxen stumbled, Uzzah reached out to steady the precarious ark and was immediately struck dead for this irreverent act. David immediately stopped the procession and transferred it to the local home of Obed-Edom the Gittite where it would remain for three months, all the time blessing this Philistine and his household.

According to the book of Chronicles, it is during this interval that David discovered the folly of his earlier attempt to move the ark (1 Chron. 15:13). Responsibility for moving the ark was the prerogative of the Levites, a principle he would have learned had he inquired of God when he began to move the ark. The informed king then, motivated by reports that the ark was bringing blessing to Obed-Edom, set out to retrieve the ark. Again, as in the first attempt, the transfer was accompanied by joyful worship and sacrifice. David, dressed in priestly clothes (a linen ephod), "danced before the LORD with all his might," surrounded by an Israelite community declaring the praise of God with shouts and music.

It is at this point that the writer of 2 Samuel again uses the foil of Saul to accentuate the character of David. This time it is Saul's daughter watching her husband David in abandoned worship before the Lord who reminds us of the contrast between David and Saul. Not only does she despise David in her heart (2 Sam. 6:16), but she confronts her husband as he enters his household, highlighting what she considers to be his vulgar behavior during the transfer of the ark (6:20). David reminds her that his behavior is defined by the theological center of his life: "It was before the LORD, who chose me rather than your father or anyone from his house when he appointed me ruler over the LORD's people Israel—I will celebrate before the LORD" (6:21). At the core of David's value system is clearly the worship of God.

DAVID INITIATES A NEW PHASE OF WORSHIP

Among the Davidic traditions in the Old Testament, it is the book of Chronicles which provides the most detail on the Davidic program of worship. David is presented in 1 Chronicles 15–16 as the founder of a new phase of worship in Israel's life.[1] This new phase, however, is carefully rooted in the earlier Mosaic tradition, and in order to highlight this the Chronicler notes several key elements of continuity. At the heart of this continuity is the ark (15:2), the sacred object which was synonymous with the presence of God. This most holy of objects in Israel's worship, to be housed in the "most holy place" of the tabernacle, was composed of the most precious materials available to Israel (Ex. 25:10–22). Its cover, called the place of atonement (Lev. 16:14), was decorated with two golden cherubim, symbolic of God's manifest presence. Exodus 25:22 makes it clear that this was the place where God would meet with his people: "I will meet with you and give you all my commands for the Israelites" (cf. 1 Chron. 13:6). But the continuity with the Mosaic phase of worship is seen also in the careful delineation of sacred personnel (Levites and priests, 15:11–15), sacred activity (sacrifices, 15:26), all linked to the sacred authority of Mosaic revelation (15:15; 16:40).

Nevertheless, alongside these elements of continuity, the Chronicler notes corresponding elements of discontinuity. A new set of sacred objects, musical instruments, is now dedicated to the worship of God (1 Chron. 15:16). There are new sacred personnel as the king dons the garments of priesthood alongside the Levitical orders (15:27) and the Levites are given a new function as they are commissioned as singers and musicians (15:16–24). Although the older sacred activity of sacrifice continues in this new phase, now this sacrifice is accompanied by music both vocal and instrumental (15:16–16:42). While the authority of the older elements of worship was clearly linked to Mosaic revelation (15:15), the authority of this new phase is linked to David (1 Chron. 15:2, 3, 11, 16; 16:4, 37, 39), who claims direct revelation from God (1 Chron. 28:11–19).

MUSICAL WORSHIP

It is evident that key to this new phase of worship initiated by David is the new sacred activity of music. In the Mosaic legislation the focus is clearly on ritual action, especially seen in the activities of sacrifice, consecration, and festal rituals, actions which are facilitated by the Levitical orders. At a few points there is evidence of a verbal aspect, whether that is related to the pronouncement of blessing (Num. 6:22–27; Deut. 10:8; 21:5) or the confession of sins (Lev. 5:5; 16:21; Num. 5:7). In the Davidic phase, however, the verbal aspect of worship is now clearly linked to music and raised to greater prominence. This greater focus on musical worship is not surprising considering David was first invited into the royal court as a harpist to soothe Saul during his attacks from the divine injurious spirit (1 Sam. 16:14–23).[2]

David's vision of worship included first the integration of a variety of musical instruments into the worship experience of Israel, including lyres, harps, cymbals, trumpets, and rams' horns (1 Chron. 15:16, 19–21, 24, 28; 16:5–6, 42). But this was not all, for the human voice was also to be featured in this new phase with the appointment of singers who were organized into choirs (15:16, 22, 27). In all of this there was a need to nurture a guild within Israel who could hone the skills necessary for this new musical phase of worship, people to whom responsibility could be given because they "were skillful at it" (15:22). For this David appointed several

Levitical families, chief among which were the families of Asaph, Heman, and Ethan (1 Chron. 15:17, 19; cf. Pss. 50, 73-83, 88, 89), each of them representing one of the main Levitical branches: Heman who is traced through Korah to Levi's son Kohath, Asaph who is traced to Levi's son Gershon, and Ethan who is traced to Levi's son Merari (1 Chron. 6:31-47).

First Chronicles 15-16 not only outlines for us the breadth of musical resources nurtured in this new phase of worship, but also the breadth of verbal expression that was commissioned by David. In 1 Chronicles 16:4 we are told that David appointed some of the Levites "to minister" before the ark of the Lord. This ministry before the ark was verbal in character and involved three types of expression: "to make petition, to give thanks, and to praise the LORD, the God of Israel." David, however, did more than just commission songs, but also created them himself, a truth reflected in the description of David in 2 Samuel 23:1 as "Israel's singer of songs."

It is interesting to note the close similarity between these three types of expression and those suggested in work on the book of Psalms. Claus Westermann boiled down the various types of psalms into two basic expressions: on the one side, those which expressed praise, and, on the other, those which expressed lament.[3] Westermann stressed, however, that even in lament the movement was always back toward praise, demonstrated by the way in which praise was a regular component of lament psalms in the Psalter. Praises in the Psalter, however, could be subdivided further into two basic types: declarative praise (thanksgiving) and descriptive praise (hymns).

However helpful, Westermann's work on the types of psalms needed further refinement and delineation, and this was accomplished brilliantly by Walter Brueggemann.[4] Brueggemann drew upon the earlier work of Paul

Ricoeur, who noted that human experience moved through a constant cycle from Orientation to Disorientation to New Orientation. Orientation typified life in equilibrium, the blessed life of promise. Disorientation typified life when this equilibrium was upset, when due to human sin or divine sovereignty difficulty was introduced into life. New Orientation typified life in transition from Disorientation back to the equilibrium of Orientation. Brueggemann wisely noted how each of the psalms can be linked to one of these points on the cycle of human experience. What were traditionally called the hymns and blessing psalms are expressions that reflect life in Orientation. What were traditionally called the laments and petition psalms are expressions that reflect life in Disorientation. What were traditionally called the thanksgiving psalms are expressions that reflect life in New Orientation. This model of categorizing the psalms is deeply rooted in the experience of God's people and reveals how the psalms have arisen out of the settings of real life with its ups and downs.

What is interesting is how this same cycle can be discerned in David's vision for worship within Israel in 1 Chronicles 16:4: to make petition (Disorientation), to give thanks (New Orientation), to praise (Orientation). Furthermore, following the appointment of the Levites to this new commission, the Chronicler includes a psalm which offers an example of the kind of expressions David had in mind. The resulting psalm is actually an amalgamation of three psalms from the Psalter: Psalm 105:1–15 (1 Chron. 16:8–22); Psalm 96:1–13 (1 Chron. 16:23–33); Psalm 106:1, 47–48 (1 Chron. 16:34–36). What is interesting is that these three psalms represent the three basic types of psalms: Psalm 105 is a psalm of thanksgiving (New Orientation), Psalm 96 is a psalm of praise (Orientation), and Psalm 106 is a psalm of penitence (Disorientation).

IMPLICATIONS

David placed worship at the center of the life of his new kingdom by bringing the ark to his capital city. He was also a catalyst for a whole new phase in worshipful expression to God with a breadth of creative musical expression both in terms of the medium of expression (instruments, voices) and the content of expression (Orientation, Disorientation, New Orientation).

These characteristics in David speak relevantly into the present context of the church. First, David reminds us that worship lies at the center of our life as the community of God. This priority is evident in John Piper's challenge to the church to make the purpose of the church not anthropocentric (the salvation of human souls), but rather theocentric (the worship of God).[5] Such a shift in perspective reminds us that the human activities of evangelism and preaching are but means to a greater end: the worship of God. When worship is subsidiary to the life of a church, that church loses its character as the community of Christ which was created to "declare the praises of him who called you out of darkness into his wonderful light" (1 Peter 2:9). The expression "to the glory of God" is often etched into the cornerstones of church buildings or slipped into mission statements as a preamble, but it needs to be evident in the life of the community both corporately and individually.

Second, the breadth of musical media in David's new phase of worship challenges us to remain open to new ways of worshiping God. For some it is easy to equate praise with the use of organ, piano, and choir, to identify true worship with these modes. For others, however, it is just as easy to equate worship with the use of drums, guitars, and worship teams and to see no value in any other forms of worship. David's new phase of worship certainly stretched his community to adopt new modes of worship, but underlying all of this there was strong evidence of joy (1 Chron. 15:16, 25), showing a people who fully embraced the new forms.

Third, the breadth of verbal content initiated by David is echoed in the New Testament witness. The early church was encouraged to echo the kind of praise initiated by David and reflected in the Psalter (Eph. 5:19; Col. 3:16; 1 Cor. 14:26). Christians were also encouraged to express their worship to God with the same breadth exhorted by David. James 5:13 encourages the early church: "Is any one of you in trouble? He should pray. Is anyone happy? Let him sing songs of praise."

What was suggested in our reading of 1 Chronicles 16 is now expressly stated: the type of expression to God is shaped by the setting of the life of God's people: in Disorientation ("Is any one of you in trouble?"), pray; in Orientation ("Is anyone happy?"), praise.

David's revolution in worship, now preserved in the Scriptures, reminds us of God's provision of a full spectrum of worshipful expression for our communion with him.[6] The church has become skilled in the expression of praise and thanksgiving in corporate settings. However, rarely are there opportunities to express pain and disillusionment along the journey of faith, even though the majority of psalms in the Psalter were written in times of Disorientation, and many of them are lament psalms expressing bold questions like "why?" and "how long?" to the Lord.[7] Such questions are often interpreted by Christians as questions of rebellion against God. However, their abundance in the Psalter suggests another explanation. Instead, these kinds of questions are expressions of a people who sincerely believe in God's promise to bless his obedient covenant children. They are a recognition of God's sovereignty over all of life and an expression of faith in God as the only source for grace.

FOR FURTHER REFLECTION

1. Think about the services at the church where you regularly attend. What is the dominant tone of the service: preaching of the Word of God, relationships with fellow Christians, evangelism of the unsaved, worship of God? These are all, unquestionably, core values of the church, as evidenced in the practice of the early church in Acts 2:42–47. However, evaluate your church in light of David's core passion of worship. Is worship important? What signals this to you? How could you make this a greater priority in your local church?

2. David introduced some innovations into the worship experience of the people of God in his day, especially the development of new media for worship. In all of this, however, this core value of worship was inextricably linked to the core value of unity (see ch. 8, "David and Unity"). How can the church embrace new media and modes of worship and yet remain united? How can you become a unifier of worship in your own local church? Pray for peace.

3. David has shown us the need for a breadth of worship expressions which reflect the breadth of the human journey with God. Brueggemann speaks of these as expressions of Orientation (praise), Disorientation (petition/lament), and New Orientation (thanksgiving). Of these psalm types, which is the most prevalent in your own individual worship of God? In your corporate worship of God? It is interesting that although the majority of psalms in the Psalter are psalms of Disorientation, most Christians find they rarely express their heart to God using the language that is found in the laments, that is, asking God questions like "why?" or "how

long?" Try to broaden the ways in which you speak to God, even in some time alone with God today. If you are a worship leader in a church, reflect on the ways in which you can incorporate the laments into the worship of your church in the coming month.

10

DAVID AND TEMPLE

It is clear from the biblical evidence that one of David's greatest passions was to build a permanent dwelling place for God in Jerusalem. We broached this subject in the previous chapter ("David and Worship"), but because among the various aspects of worship this may have been David's greatest innovation to the Mosaic legislation, we will devote an entire chapter to this subject.

THE TABERNACLE AND
THE PRESENCE OF GOD

At Sinai God revealed through Moses the stipulations for the tabernacle, the purposes for which were made clear at the outset of this legislation in Exodus 25:8–9: "Then have them make a sanctuary for me, and I will dwell among them. Make this tabernacle and all its furnishings exactly like the pattern I will show you." The purpose of the tabernacle was to make possible the dwelling of the Lord God among his people.

The difficulty this entailed is made clear in the initial encounter between God and his people on Mount Sinai (Ex. 19–20). The people were consecrated in preparation for the appearance of the Lord, and his arrival is described in the following way:

> On the morning of the third day there was thunder and lightning, with a thick cloud over the mountain, and a very loud trumpet blast. Everyone in the camp trembled. Then Moses led the people out of the camp to meet with God, and they stood at the foot of the mountain. Mount Sinai was covered with smoke, because the LORD descended on it in fire. The smoke billowed up from it like smoke from a furnace, the whole mountain trembled violently, and the sound of the trumpet grew louder and louder. (Ex. 19:16–19)

The people were warned not only to avoid any contact with or sight of God, but also to avoid any contact with the mountain itself. It is not surprising then that, following God's pronouncement of the Ten Commandments in Exodus 20:1–17, the people would tremble with fear, remain at a distance, and request that Moses be their mediator from this point forth (Ex. 20:18–19). Such an experience would have highlighted the clear difference between these divine and human partners in this new covenant relationship. How then will this people relate to their God whose holiness is not only terrifying but life-threatening?

The answer to this question is the focus of much of the latter section of the book of Exodus, that is, the tabernacle instruction found in Exodus 25–40. The fulfillment of the purpose of this tabernacle (25:8–9) is described in the final paragraph of the book: "Then the cloud covered the Tent of Meeting, and the glory of the LORD filled the tabernacle. Moses could not enter the Tent of Meeting because the cloud had settled upon it, and the glory of the LORD filled the tabernacle" (Ex. 40:34–35). Through the tabernacle the holy and transcendent Creator made possible his immanent dwelling among his creation. By using a tent, he was truly dwelling among his people, who likewise were living in tents for their sojourn from Egypt to Canaan.

DAVID'S PASSION FOR A TEMPLE

The tabernacle would continue as the dwelling place of God for Israel throughout the period prior to the monarchy, stationed first at Shiloh (1 Sam. 1–2), then later at Nob (1 Sam. 21–22) and Gibeon (1 Chron. 16:39; 2 Chron. 1:3–6). The tabernacle's existence, however, suggests a people still not fully settled in this land of promise. That this typifies the period up until David's time can be discerned in God's promise to David in 2 Samuel 7:10–11 (cf. //1 Chronicles 17:9–10):

> And I will provide a place for my people Israel and will plant them so that they can have a home of their own and no longer be disturbed. Wicked people will not oppress them anymore, as they did at the beginning and have done ever since the time I appointed leaders [literally, "judges"] over my people Israel. I will also give you rest from all your enemies.

And so David expressed his passion for a permanent dwelling place for God in Jerusalem (2 Sam. 7:1–2). The Lord, however, does not grant David permission to build the temple, the reason for which is related in later passages to David's lack of peace (1 Kings 5:3) and his role in battle (1 Chron. 22:8; 28:3). Instead God designates David's son (Solomon) as the one who would be granted this commission (2 Sam. 7:12–13//1 Chron. 17:11–12).

Nevertheless, David was instrumental in preparing his kingdom and his successor to build this temple. He purchased the site of the temple from Araunah the Jebusite

(2 Sam. 24//1 Chron. 21), demanding that the price be set at a premium ("the full price," 1 Chron. 21:22), so that there would be no question that it was in Israelite hands prior to the construction, and also that it was David who had provided the site for the temple.

Although David would not build the temple proper, he would provide an altar of sacrifice on the site, an act that highlights one of the core functions of the temple within the community of Israel (see ch. 12, "David and Sin"). Again, as with the temple site, so with the first sacrifice that was offered on that altar David demanded to pay "the full price," refusing to "sacrifice a burnt offering that costs me nothing" (2 Sam. 24:24//1 Chron. 21:24).

While the book of Samuel does not offer any more detail on David's contribution to the temple project, the Chronicler includes several chapters outlining the intricate preparations David undertook, ranging from the appointment of personnel (builders, priests) to the provision of materials to the articulation of plans (1 Chron. 22–29).

David's reason for these extensive preparations is linked to the contrast between the youth and inexperience of his heir apparent Solomon and the high standard of "magnificence and fame and splendor" required for the temple which would stand out "in the sight of all the nations" (1 Chron. 22:5). But according to the Chronicler, David did not pursue this preparation alone. He called on all the leaders of Israel to help Solomon. Involvement in the construction of the temple, however, was no mere political act for David. According to 1 Chronicles 22:19, there is an important fusion between the building of the sanctuary of the Lord God and the full devotion of one's heart and soul to seek the Lord. For David the physical construction of this temple was an expression of his passionate commitment to the Lord.

The Chronicler relates explicitly that David's plans for the temple were not personal preferences but rather direct revelation from the Spirit of God, as 1 Chronicles 28:12 asserts: "[David] gave [Solomon] the plans of all that the Spirit had put in his mind," plans which David had "in writing from the hand of the LORD upon me" (v. 19). Even the understanding of the details of these plans was provided by God to David. David's parting words to the assembly make clear the purpose of this project: "The task is great, because this palatial structure is not for human beings but for the LORD God" (1 Chron. 29:1). The building of the temple would then be an extension of David's passionate worship of the Lord God, and those who join the project would need to be consecrated as if they are serving as priests in the house (1 Chron. 29:5).

One of the Chronicler's last scenes in David's life depicts a great event of sacrifice at the altar which marked the site of the future temple. The number of sacrifices is gargantuan with bulls, rams, male lambs as well as drink offerings and other sacrifices (1 Chron 29:21–22). The final words, however, set the tone for the function of the temple: "They ate and drank with great joy in the presence of the LORD that day."

The temple ultimately would function as a place of fellowship, as the people joyously feasted with their God. Although David would never see the fruit of his preparations, he is described in Chronicles as a leader passionate to see the permanent dwelling of God manifest among his adoring people.

THE TEMPLE AS A PLACE OF PRAYER

After David's death, the temple would finally replace the tabernacle, and once again the Lord would fill the temple with his glory, presencing himself with his people (1 Kings 8:10–13). The description bears striking similarity to the description of God filling the tabernacle in

Exodus 40: "When the priests withdrew from the Holy Place, the cloud filled the temple of the LORD. And the priests could not perform their service because of the cloud, for the glory of the LORD filled his temple" (1 Kings 8:10–11).

As the replacement for the tabernacle, signaled by the transportation of the ark into the temple structure (1 Kings 8:1–9), the temple would now be the location at which the priestly sacrifices would be offered. This role is inaugurated at the dedication of the temple as the king and his people offer burnt, grain, and fellowship offerings to the Lord (1 Kings 9:62–64). Nevertheless, Solomon's great prayer at the dedication of the temple places greater emphasis on the temple as a place of prayer.

This prayer, 1 Kings 8:22–61, begins and ends by rehearsing the gracious character and action of the Lord toward his people. The Lord is a God unparalleled in the world who is faithful to his covenant of love (v. 23). The two covenants that are accentuated are the covenant with David which made possible this temple (vv. 24–26) and the covenant with Israel through Moses that made possible this people (vv. 52–53). Because of this covenantal relationship, Solomon asks this heavenly God, whose presence no temple could contain or restrict, to listen to the prayers that are prayed in and toward this temple in the years to come. Solomon lists the many circumstances in which the people will find themselves, and in each case shows how they will cry out to God toward this temple. He implores God to hear these prayers, to forgive his people, and to save them from their predicament.

Whereas the greater focus with the tabernacle was on sacrifice, an equal if not greater focus of the temple would be on prayer. The temple would nurture the relationship between God and his people, especially when they have strayed from covenant faithfulness.

DAVID'S TEMPLE, MESSIAH,
AND THE CHURCH

Solomon's hope for this "magnificent temple" was that it would be "a place for you to dwell forever" (1 Kings 8:13). However, this would not be realized. The disobedience of future generations of Davidic kings and their people would so offend the Lord and stain the land, the city, and even the temple itself that God would abandon the temple. The tragedy of Ezekiel's ministry was that he had to watch the glory of God depart from the temple (Ezek. 10), an excruciating scene for one designated as a priest (Ezek. 1:3). Nevertheless, Ezekiel envisioned a day when this glory will return to the temple (Ezek. 43). This return of glory is not related in the rest of the Old Testament.[1]

It is interesting that when Messiah Jesus comes, John describes the event in similar terms to the tabernacle of old (John 1:14): "The Word became flesh and made his dwelling [tabernacled] among us. We have seen his glory, the glory of the One and Only, who came from the Father full of grace and truth." In Exodus 33:19–20 the Lord tells Moses that he cannot see him lest he die, and when the Lord does pass by him the words ring out: "abounding in love and faithfulness" = full of grace and truth (Ex. 34:6). Christ refers to himself as the temple. Standing before the second temple in John 2:19–22 he challenges the Jews to "destroy this temple, and I will raise it again in three days." The Jews think he speaks of the physical temple, but John tells us that "the temple he had spoken of was his body."

As the place of God's dwelling (temple or tabernacle), Christ is the way of access to God's presence. The goal of David's temple is the goal of the incarnation: the Lord dwelling on earth with humans in the fullness of his attributes. But there is more. The apostle Paul also speaks of us as Christians as the "temple of God," the temple of the

Holy Spirit. In a way unique from the Israelites of old, God's presence would fill our lives (1 Cor. 3:16; 6:15, 19).

On a final note, as we look to the eschatological destination of this theme, it is interesting that in the New Jerusalem there will be no temple, because the Lord God Almighty and the Lamb are its temple (Rev. 21:22). This speaks to the ultimate experience of a face-to-face relationship with the Lord.

As we catalogue David's passionate agenda for the temple, we see more than just the construction of a physical building. Rather, as the scene in 1 Chronicles 29 confirms, it is an agenda of relationship with the God of Israel who blesses this people with his manifest presence in their midst. So as Jesus comes to bring God's presence on earth, he functions as a Davidic royal, but now with a twist. He himself now replaces the physical temple as the place of God's manifest presence. Through him we now may approach God without even the barriers of holy space.

Furthermore, as followers of Messiah Jesus we now are a temple community in which can be found the manifest presence of the Divine King. Such a truth reminds us of the incredible blessing we have received at this climactic moment in redemptive history. At the same time, it has serious ramifications for our lives. The apostle Paul reminds us that the indwelling Spirit will mean that we will begin to reflect the Lord's glory, which means we will be increasingly transformed into his likeness (2 Cor. 3:7–18). As the temple was a place of consecration and ritual purity, so the messianic community must now reflect such consecration and purity. This means then rejection of impure pursuits, participation in which would be unimaginable in the temple precincts (1 Cor. 6:19).

David's passion for the temple is an expression of his deep love and devotion to God, and so the new temple of the church must be known for its passionate abandon to the worship of the Lord who stoops to indwell his redeemed people.

FOR FURTHER REFLECTION

1. The temple should prompt us to thank God for the gift of his son who "tabernacled" among us and through whom we have access to God because of faith.

2. The tabernacle and the temple and their common scenes of God's manifest presence descending into the structures remind us of the holy presence of God. In each case people are forced away from the place of God's manifest presence because of its dangerous character. There are times that, as Christians who celebrate the reality that through and in Christ we have access to God's presence as his children, we become complacent and even flippant in our approach to God. It is important that we first celebrate the amazing character of the incarnation and of the access we enjoy through Christ's death and resurrection. While we revel in the fact that we can address God as Abba, it is also important to revisit passages like Hebrews 12:28–29 which remind us that we are to "worship God acceptably with reverence and awe, for our 'God is a consuming fire'" (citing Deut. 4:24). We cannot forget that God is the holy Other, that apart from Jesus we have no hope to enter his brilliant presence.

3. Solomon identifies the temple as a place of prayer and petition, reminding us of God's desire to meet us, to commune with us, and to hear our needs. A great emphasis in Solomon's prayer, however, is upon the confession of sin by an unfaithful people. God invites us back to covenant relationship, and Solomon's prayer offers us a way of expressing our heart to God in contrition. Reveling in the grace of God, we often take sin lightly, but Solomon here revels in the grace of God (expressed through his

emphasis on the covenant of love at the outset of the prayer) as a foundation for confessing our sins to God. This echoes the declaration of Paul that "God's kindness leads you toward repentance" (Rom. 2:4) and the promise of 1 John 1:9 that "if we confess our sins, he is faithful and just and will forgive us our sins and purify us from all unrighteousness." Take some time to cry to God in humble penitence, because of his grace expressed through Jesus.

4. If we as believers are truly the fulfillment of the temple, in what ways have you seen evidence of the presence of God in your own life individually, but also in the life of your community of faith?

II

DAVID AND FAITHFULNESS

There is little question that the writer of Samuel brings great focus on the friendship between Jonathan and David in order to accentuate the enmity between Jonathan's father Saul and David. While Saul becomes increasingly jealous and violent toward the young David, Jonathan's commitment only deepens.[1] The focus on the relationship between Jonathan and David receives so much attention in the narrative of Samuel that it takes on a life of its own and highlights another important value in the Davidic tradition, that of covenant faithfulness.

DAVID AND JONATHAN

The narrative clearly attributes to Jonathan the initiative in this relationship, not surprising considering that at the outset at least Jonathan was socially superior as the king's favored son. In the first description of their relationship Jonathan is the subject of all the actions: he "became one in spirit with David . . . loved him as himself . . . made a covenant with David because he loved him as himself . . . took off the robe he was wearing . . . gave it to David along with his tunic . . . sword . . . bow . . . belt"

(1 Sam. 18:1–4). Packed into these short verses are expressions denoting deep intimacy. To become one in spirit is a translation of the phrase more woodenly translated as "the soul of Jonathan was bound together with the soul of David." This verb "bound together" (*qashar*) is used to refer to the literal action of tying (Gen. 38:28; Jer. 51:63) or binding materials together (Neh. 3:38), but can have a metaphorical sense of "being in league, conspiring with" (e.g., 2 Sam. 15:31). Here it describes Jonathan as David's "bosom buddy." This is expressed also in terms of the quality of love that Jonathan had for David: "he loved him as himself," a phrase that appears several times in the David-Jonathan narratives (1 Sam. 18:3; 20:17). The offer of his royal clothing and weaponry is the first sign that Jonathan is deferring to David not just as the true crown prince, but the legitimate king of Israel, a truth he will finally embrace in 1 Samuel 23:16–18.[2]

That this relationship is more than temporary is made clear by the reference to his making of "a covenant" with David. A covenant or *berith* is an agreement with obligation between two parties and is used regularly to structure the relationship between God and humanity, especially as evidenced in the covenants of Noah, Abraham, Sinai, and David (see ch. 4, "David and Covenant"). However, covenants were also used in relationships between humans as demonstrated in such passages as Genesis 14:13 (Abraham and the Amorites), 31:44–55 (Jacob and Laban), Joshua 9 (Israel and the Gibeonites), and 2 Samuel 3:21 (king and people).

The use of a covenant suggests a careful consideration of the relationship between two parties. This covenant brought structure and formalization to the relationship between Jonathan and David. However, such a covenant did not diminish the depth of emotional connection between the two young men as is made clear in nearly every description of their relationship. After Saul commanded Jonathan to kill David in 19:1, we are told that Jonathan took great delight in David (cf. the use of this Hebrew phrase in negative and positive ways in 2 Sam. 15:26; Mal. 2:17). After Jonathan warns David of Saul's anger and encourages him to flee the court, we are told that they kissed each other and wept deeply, actions signaling a depth of commitment reserved elsewhere for extraordinary greetings or farewells between members of the same gender within a family unit (Gen. 33:4; 45:15; 50:1; Ruth 1:9, 14).[3] Finally, after the death of Jonathan in 2 Samuel 1:25–27 David wails: "I grieve for you, Jonathan my brother; you were very dear to me. Your love for me was wonderful, more wonderful than that of women." These examples reveal a level of intimacy and friendship that is unprecedented in the Old Testament.[4]

Such initiative from Jonathan was deemed folly by Saul, who would eventually warn his son that David would steal the kingdom from Jonathan (1 Sam. 20:31). And it is in this context that we see the climactic expression of their covenant commitment to one another. In 1 Samuel 20 David is justifiably afraid that Saul will kill him at the approaching New Moon festival, an event which is about to take place on the first few days of the approaching month (Num. 10:10; 28:11–15). Jonathan agrees to gauge his father's intentions for David, concocting an intricate plan to signal David. The key to this passage, however, is not the plan itself, but the language of mutual relationship that is expressed throughout.

In 20:8 David pleads with Jonathan to remain faithful to the commitment he had made at the outset of their relationship: "show kindness to your servant for you have brought him into a covenant with you before the LORD." Here we learn that the covenant which Jonathan made with David (18:3) was not merely an agreement on the horizontal level (human-human) but had a vertical dimension as well, for it was "a covenant with you before the LORD" (lit., a covenant of the LORD with you). This vertical dimension is not odd in ancient agreements, for it was common that the deity would be called upon as witness to the agreement between covenant parties, something that can be discerned later in verse 23 when Jonathan says, "The LORD is witness between you and me forever," and in his closing speech of verse 42 when he declares: "we have sworn friendship with each other in the name of the LORD, saying, 'The LORD is witness between you and me.'" But there is more here than the regular divine witness in covenant agreements, and this is made clear in Jonathan's response to David in verse 14: "show me unfailing kindness like that of the LORD." The Lord is thus not only witness to this covenant, uniquely positioned to ensure fidelity by both partners through all generations, but he is also the exemplar of the core value that ensures the endurance of such covenant relationships.

This core value is singled out in the speech of both David and Jonathan as "kindness" (vv. 8, 14–15). In Hebrew the term is *hesedh*, a word which describes the loyalty expected of those who have entered into covenant relationship. This term is used consistently of God's loyalty to his covenant people and appears regularly in the phrase which is often translated as "to keep covenant of love" and appears in the core recitations of God's character in the Old Testament (Ex. 20:6; 34:6–7). The source of the "kindness," or better, covenant faithfulness, thus is the Lord himself, which is why Jonathan qualifies it as "like that of the LORD" in 1 Samuel 20:14. The Old Testament elsewhere makes clear that this characteristic of the Lord was to be evident in God's people (Hos. 6:6; 10:12; 12:6; Mic. 6:8; cf. 2 Sam. 9:1), even if they rarely lived up to this ideal (Hos. 4:1; 6:4).

There is record of only one encounter between David and Jonathan after this point. In 1 Samuel 23:15–18, David is hiding from Saul in the wilderness of Ziph, and Jonathan finds him at his hiding place. We are told that there he "helped him find strength in God" (lit., strengthened his hands in God). Jonathan, the bosom buddy bound together in spirit in God's presence and according to his character, appears at a moment of great despair to encourage his friend. The encouragement is partially prophetic: Saul will not find David and David will become king. However, one aspect would never be realized: Jonathan would never again be next to David. This final experience is commemorated with the renewal of their covenant before the Lord, before they part for the last time.

The relationship between David and Jonathan is a powerful witness to the depth of intimacy that can be shared between two human beings. However, such depth is possible only as we are accountable to the Lord as covenant guarantor and as we participate in his divine nature (2 Peter 1:4).

DAVID AND MEPHIBOSHETH

While the covenant made between David and Jonathan had implications for their own relationship, their speeches reveal that it also had ramifications for the future. It is Jonathan who voices this in 1 Samuel 20:14–15. He requests David's *hesedh* not only throughout his lifetime ("as long as I live, so that I may not be killed," v. 14), but also for generations to come ("do not ever cut off your kindness from my family," v. 15). Furthermore, Jonathan's speech to David speaks of the Lord's witness to the oath made not only between the two of them, but also "between your descendants and my descendants forever" (v. 42). This is why the writer of the book of Samuel refers to Jonathan's agreement as making "a covenant with the house of David" (v. 16).

After 1 Samuel 20 Jonathan largely disappears from the account of David, except for the short encouragement already noted in 1 Samuel 23:15–18 and the account of his death with Saul and his brothers in battle in 1 Samuel 31. However, as mentioned, the covenant was not buried with Jonathan, but lived on in perpetuity. Even so, the text of 2 Samuel gives few indications of any future implications. There is an odd passing reference in 2 Samuel 4:4 to the survival of a descendant of Jonathan, that is, his son Mephibosheth (also known as Meribbaal)[5] who was crippled in his feet when his nurse dropped him when fleeing after the death of Jonathan at Mount Gilboa. This reference is overshadowed in its present context by the death of Ish-bosheth, the final blow to the power of the family of Saul, after which David had full control of the kingdom.

The writer of the book of Samuel, however, is not finished with Jonathan and his family, and this passing reference foreshadows a key incident which is related in 2 Samuel 9. Once David has firmly established his rule and has entered into covenant with the Lord, he sets out to fulfill the covenant agreement he had made with Jonathan in 1 Samuel 20, desirous to find someone from Saul's family "to whom I can show kindness for Jonathan's sake" (2 Sam. 9:1). To pursue this he summons the former servant of Saul's household, Ziba, and through him discovers that the lame Mephibosheth remains alive. David restores Saul's lands and servants to Mephibosheth and invites him to eat at the king's table for the rest of his life.

David explicitly relates this action to the covenant he had secured with Jonathan, not only when he uses the language "for Jonathan's sake" (9:1) and "for the sake of your father Jonathan" (9:7), but more importantly when he speaks of showing kindness, that is, *hesedh* toward Mephibosheth (9:1, 3, 7). A close look at David's words, however, emphasizes again an important aspect evident in the original covenant declarations between David and Jonathan.

The first time David phrases his question (9:1) he says: "Is there anyone still left of the house of Saul to whom I can show kindness for Jonathan's sake?" However, the second time he modifies the question slightly (9:3): "Is there no one still left of the house of Saul to whom I can show God's kindness?" The addition of the possessive "God's" highlights the intimate connection between divine and human *hesedh*. For David to act faithfully toward Mephibosheth was nothing less than for God himself to act faithfully toward Mephibosheth. By fulfilling covenant with Jonathan's descendants, David is embodying the faithful character of God himself, as Jonathan had said "show me unfailing kindness *like that of the LORD*" (1 Sam. 20:14).

David had no need politically to follow through on his commitments to Jonathan and, if anything, it was dangerous to reinstate Mephibosheth's economic power and political status, something that would become apparent during Absalom's revolt (2 Sam. 16:1–4; 19:24–30).[6] But he did so because he had first learned such precarious faithfulness from his soul friend, Jonathan, who in turn was reflecting the character of the covenant Lord of Israel.

IMPLICATIONS

Christ

The gospel of John describes Jesus (the Word) as the one who embodied the very character of God; he was "full of grace and truth," a phrase that contains an echo of the words of God's self-disclosure found in Exodus 34:6: "abounding in love [*hesedh*] and faithfulness." In a truly unique way Jesus embodied the *hesedh* character of the Lord, covenant faithfulness that would ultimately lead him to the cross. The gospel writer signals that the ultimate expression of covenant fidelity is found in the cross when he writes in John 13:1: "Jesus knew that the time had come for him to leave this world and go to the Father. Having loved his own who were in the world, he now showed them the full extent of his love." The ultimacy of this act of love is repeated in John 15:13 which declares: "Greater love has no one than this: to lay down one's life for one's friends" (TNIV).

Christian

The kind of covenant fidelity that Christ expressed in his life and climactically in his death is also demanded of us as his followers. This is expressed most consistently in the Johannine tradition in the New Testament through which Christ expresses his "new commandment": "As I have loved you, so you must love one another" (John 13:34; 15:12, 17; 1 John 2:7–8; 3:11, 23; 2 John 5). That love lies at the core of the Christian ethic is seen in its ubiquitous appearance throughout biblical revelation (Lev. 19:18; Matt. 5:44; Gal. 5:14; Eph. 5:2; 1 Thess. 4:9; Heb. 13:1; 1 Peter 1:22; 1 John 4:7, 10–11). Such expression of covenant fidelity to one another also has the potential of impacting a watching world, as John 13:35 declares: "By this everyone will know that you are my disciples, if you love one another."

Thus the covenant faithfulness of God that underlies and is expressed in the relationship between Jonathan and David, is the same covenant faithfulness that David's son Jesus expressed and taught on earth. He calls us as his community to express and teach this same love that the world may know and experience the riches of God's covenant faithfulness.

FOR FURTHER REFLECTION

1. Compare the quality of friendship you enjoy with your closest friend (nonfamily) and the quality of friendship that was shared between David and Jonathan. Resolve to speak with this person this

week either to deepen your friendship and/or to thank that person for the friendship you have enjoyed over the years.

2. The triangulation of David, God, and Jonathan reminds us that our relationships with one another must have a spiritual dimension. Celebrate those relationships that include this dimension and think of ways you can incorporate such a dimension into those that lack it.

3. David saw his expression of covenant faithfulness to Mephibosheth as nothing less than an expression of God's faithfulness. Identify someone in your sphere of life and influence to whom you can practically show God's faithfulness this week and take steps to carry it out.

12

DAVID AND SIN

Second Samuel 11 marks a critical juncture in the account of David as king over all Israel in the books of Samuel (2 Sam. 5–10). Except for the tragic death of Uzzah in the first attempt to move the ark (2 Sam. 6:1–11), to this point the narrative has been entirely positive, with David embraced by Israel, victorious in battle, rewarded by God, and described as faithful and just. However, from 2 Samuel 11 on, the narrative shifts almost exclusively to the mood of tragedy and disaster.

DAVID, BATHSHEBA, AND URIAH

This downward spiral is inaugurated by the infamous story of David, Bathsheba, and Uriah. The narrator of the event suggests at the outset that David's presence in Jerusalem in the springtime was abnormal for it was "the time when kings go off to war" (11:1).[1] While Joab, David's general, was off leading the army, David was in his capital city. And it was during this time that one evening David, from his vantage point in one of the taller structures of the city, spied the beautiful Bathsheba bathing. The rest of the story is well known: he sleeps with the married woman, she conceives, he tries to cover it up by enticing Uriah to sleep with his wife, but failing this, ends up arranging for his soldier's death in the front lines. Clearly the narrator contrasts the faithful Uriah with the unfaithful David as twice Uriah refuses to sleep with his wife while his military colleagues remain in battle.

Writers of Old Testament narratives rarely explicitly state their evaluation of the event they are relating. Instead, they will use various narrative techniques to communicate what is often called the "ideological point of view."[2] There are a few cases where they use "authorial assertion," that is, explicit statements by the narrator evaluating the story for the reader. More common, however, are techniques like providing the speech of an authoritative character in the story, like a prophet, priest, or sage, describing the outcome of the story, or even arranging the details of the story to suggest an evaluation.

The narrator of 2 Samuel 11 takes no chances on misinterpretation by using every technique available to offer a negative evaluation of David's actions. He arranges the details of the story to contrast David with Uriah, highlighting through this the unfaithfulness of David. Additionally, the outcome of the story makes it clear that David has sinned greatly against God and humanity: a married woman is pregnant by a man other than her husband, and her husband, a faithful soldier, lies dead because of the murderous plot of the man who impregnated his wife. But if this is not enough, the narrator also includes the encounter between the prophet Nathan and the guilty David in 2 Samuel 12, making clear God's judgment of David's action. And finally, if the reader has missed all of these clues, the narrator includes the declarative narrative of 11:27 where he asserts: "the thing David had done displeased the LORD."

Such a thorough evaluation of an event brings great attention on these scenes in 2 Samuel 11–12 and rightfully so, since it marks the beginning of an avalanche of calamity that will befall David and his family. The child born to Bathsheba would die within seven days of his birth. David's son Amnon would rape his half sister Tamar (2 Sam. 13), and her brother Absalom would kill Amnon in revenge (2 Sam. 13). Absalom would plot his father's demise and even take over the kingdom for a period, but ultimately this scheme would fail and Absalom would die (2 Sam. 14–19). After the death of Absalom, the Benjaminite Sheba would rebel against David and lead the northern tribes out from under David's control, a reminder of the tenuousness of David's united kingdom (2 Sam. 20).

The flow of the narrative in 2 Samuel 11–20 demonstrates the awful consequences of the sin of David and the impact such a sin had on his family and kingdom. Nevertheless, it also provides an opportunity to examine more closely the response of both God and David to the failures of the king. It is often in the midst of failure that we find out much about a person and God. In order to do this, a closer look at two passages that bracket this latter phase of the account of David's life is in order.

DAVID THE CONFESSOR

The prophet Nathan's speech to David in 2 Samuel 12 is one of the shrewdest confrontations in the Bible. David was accustomed to ruling on cases in his royal court (see ch. 7, "David and Justice"), and so Nathan begins by weaving a story that would have suggested to David that he was to rule on a dispute between two people in his kingdom. Nathan describes a scenario in which a rich flock owner unjustly uses the lone precious sheep of a poor man in order to entertain a visitor. David took the bait, quickly and passionately announcing judgment on the rich man, only to learn that he had just condemned himself, as Nathan accuses: "You are the man!"

The prophetic speech which follows is structured into three parts. First, God reviews the history of his relationship with

David (12:7–8), a section which is typical of covenant material and which echoes the foundational covenant–making speech of 2 Samuel 7 (see ch. 4, "David and Covenant"). Second, God's question, "Why did you despise the word of the LORD by doing what is evil in his eyes?" introduces the list of violations committed by David (12:9). Finally (introduced by the phrase, "Now, therefore . . . "), the judgment is pronounced, and the judgment is directly related to his sin (12:10–12). Nathan announces to him that as he used the sword to kill Uriah, so "the sword will never depart from your house," and that as he slept with another man's wife, so "one who is close to you . . . will lie with your wives."

Our last glimpse of David was in 12:5–6 as he angrily bursts forth with his judgment on a scenario he thought unrelated to his own life. But Nathan's speech has stripped him of such anger and replaced it with nothing but guilt. The words of the humbled king are simple, but essential: "I have sinned against the LORD" (12:13). Here is the quality that distinguishes David from Saul and makes him "a man after [God's] own heart" (1 Sam. 13:14). When confronted by the prophet Samuel, Saul is quick to justify his actions (1 Sam. 13:11–12; 15:10–23), and only after elongated debate and the announcement of the rejection of God does he finally cry: "I have sinned" (1 Sam. 15:24–25, 30). In contrast, David responds immediately with his admission of guilt.

Nathan's response to David is swift and reveals the balance between grace and discipline that is evident throughout all of Scripture. He announces absolution ("the LORD has taken away your sin") and promises that God will not end David's life, even though he has taken the life of another man (Ex. 21:12). Nevertheless, there are consequences for his sin, the first of which will be the death of the child conceived by David and Bathsheba. Furthermore, the narratives which follow in 2 Samuel 13–20 reveal that God's sentence in 12:10–12 will become reality for David's family and kingdom.

DAVID THE MEDIATOR

First Samuel 11 and 12 introduce us to David as sinner before God and are followed by the sequence of events that befell David's family and kingdom in the wake of his failure. At the end of this sequence appears a second key passage which again reminds us of his frailty as a human being and his desperate need for God's grace.

Second Samuel 24 narrates the dire consequences of David's decision to take a census of the military potential of Israel and Judah. It is never stated explicitly why assessing military potential was inappropriate for Israel, but it may be related to the need for Israel to rely on God for their military power and victory or to the promise that the number of descendants of Abraham would be uncountable (Gen. 12:2; 15:5; 1 Chron. 27:23). The text does claim that David was incited to do this because of God's anger against Israel, and it is assumed that such anger had been aroused because of the disobedience of the nation.[3] Here we see then disobedience on the part of both people and leader.

The inappropriateness of David's action is highlighted by Joab's attempts to dissuade the king, but the general is unsuccessful, and so for over nine months he and his army commanders spread out across Israel to count the fighting men and report the number to David (24:3–9).[4] Unlike the Bathsheba incident, however, David is stricken in his conscience (lit., "the heart of David struck him")[5] before any prophetic confrontation, and he again cries to God: "I have sinned greatly in what I have done. Now, O LORD, I beg you, take away the guilt of your servant. I have a done a very foolish thing" (24:10). Gad, the prophet in the royal court ("David's seer," 24:11), was sent with God's reply, which gives David three options of discipline: three years of famine, three months of flight from his enemies, or three days of plague.

David's response is based upon his understanding of God's mercy: "Let us fall into the hands of the LORD, for his mercy is great," and so the three-day plague is sent from God. It ravaged the entire land of Israel ("from Dan to Beersheba," that is, from the far northern Dan to the far southern Beersheba) and then moved finally to destroy Jerusalem. At this point, however, we are told that "the LORD was grieved because of the calamity and said to the angel who was afflicting the people, 'Enough! Withdraw your hand'" (24:16).

The reason for God's grief has been foreshadowed in David's statement about the greatness of the Lord's mercy. But what is now revealed in 24:17–25 is the crucial role that David played in bringing an end to the punishment. As David observed the suffering of his people, he declared to God that since it was he who was responsible for this punishment, the punishment should be restricted to "me and my family" (24:17).[6] This substitutionary offer was courageous on David's part and revealed his love and care for the people, but was rejected by the Lord. Instead, David was instructed to build an altar on "the threshing floor of Araunah the Jebusite" (24:18). The king approached Araunah to negotiate the purchase of this divinely selected site, but the non-Israelite,[7] as a gesture of respect and submission, offered the threshing floor, oxen, and wood without charge. David, however, refused, insisting he pay for the site since he would "not sacrifice to the LORD my God burnt offerings that cost me nothing" (24:24). There David built an altar, offered sacrifices to the Lord, prompting the gracious grief of God (24:16) to answer David's prayer and stop the devastating plague.

The significance of this event transcends the immediate circumstances of the census and the plague. The event highlights the principles of mediation and sacrifice. These principles are emphasized even more poignantly in the Davidic tradition in the books of Chronicles, for the altar on this threshing floor is identified as the site where Solomon's temple was built (1 Chron. 22:1; 2 Chron. 3:1). David's mediation and sacrifice reveal the priestly role that he played even as king, a role that is highlighted in Psalm 110 where he is linked to Melchizedek, the priest-king who predated David in the city of Jerusalem (see ch. 5, "David and Rule"). There is no denying that David was a sinner before God and that his sins had a damaging effect upon his nation and family. However, even his sin has a redemptive quality, for through it we see more clearly the mercy of God that was experienced through sacrifice.

These two events of sin serve as bookends on a painful chapter of the story of David. Another perspective on his struggle with sin which offers a way forward for those of us following in David's path is offered through Psalm 51, to which we now turn.

PSALM 51

The superscription of Psalm 51 connects this psalm of penitence to the historical setting of David's sin against Bathsheba. The psalm begins with the request that lies at the heart of the psalm, the impassioned cry both for mercy and for cleansing from sin, divine actions that are in turn linked to the divine characteristics of "unfailing love" (*hesedh*) and "great compassion" (*rov rahamim*). Such characteristics lie at the heart of God's self-revelation throughout the history of God's people as can be seen in Exodus 34:6–7 (cf. 33:19); Numbers 14:18; 2 Chronicles 30:9; Nehemiah 9:17; Psalms 86:15; 103:8; 111:4; 145:8; Joel 2:13; Jonah 4:2; Nahum 1:3. What is fascinating is that the majority of these contexts are related to the issue of sin: whether that is repentance/renewal (2 Chron. 30:9; Joel 2:13), forgiveness (Ex. 34:6–7; Jonah 4:2; Num. 14:18; Neh. 9:17; Pss. 86:15; 103:8), or punishment (Nah. 1:3).[8]

This is seen most poignantly in the revelation of Exodus 34 which comes in response to the people's great sin with the golden calf at Mount Sinai.

These same characteristics lie at the heart of David's relationship with God in the narratives of the books of Samuel. It is *hesedh* that undergirds God's eternal covenant with David (2 Sam. 7:15; see ch. 4, "David and Covenant") and *hesedh* that guides David's relationships with others (2 Sam. 9; see ch. 11, "David and Faithfulness"). In 2 Samuel 24:14, David elects the plague as punishment for his folly, because this would place him directly into the disciplinary hands of the Lord whose "mercies are great" (*rov rahamim*).

These aspects of God's character invoked in Psalm 51 make possible his actions of grace. The first, "to have mercy," denotes the disposition of God toward the supplicant, that is, "to favor someone," while the others (blot out, wash away, cleanse) all denote the covering or removal of sin from the supplicant. The first speaks to God's relationship to the supplicant, while the others to the supplicant's sin. This sin is described with the full range of vocabulary available to the psalmist, transgression (*pesha'*), iniquity (*'awon*), sin (*hatta'th*), terms piled up to express the greatness of the sin both in quality and quantity. These opening two verses demonstrate that forgiveness is found at the intersection of divine grace and human sinfulness.

Key to forgiveness is the acknowledgment of human sinfulness and divine justice, and this is the focus of verses 3–6 in the psalm. The psalmist does not try to hide his sin but rather acknowledges its pervasive presence not only in the current circumstances, but also from the very beginning of his life. The consistency of his sinful acts reveals a disposition of sinfulness. Not denying the impact of his sin on fellow humanity, the psalmist emphasizes the divine dimension of all sin. In David's case, underlying his violation of Bathsheba and murder of Uriah was his complete disregard for the unprecedented covenant of grace that God had established with him (2 Sam. 7). Just as David's acts of covenant loyalty (*hesedh*) to Jonathan and his family were expressions of the covenant loyalty of the Lord (see ch. 11, "David and Faithfulness"), so David's acts of covenant disloyalty (sin) against Bathsheba and Uriah were expressions of covenant disloyalty against the Lord.

This section not only acknowledges the reality of human sinfulness, but also acknowledges God's right to announce judgment and enact justice. The psalmist is aware that God's confrontation is not only completely justified, but also necessary for the resolution of his present predicament. Such confrontation involves God piercing to the innermost recesses of our lives where he desires honest truth and wisdom, the first step toward reconciliation.

Having acknowledged his sin and God's justice, the psalmist then presents his request proper to God in verses 7–12, expanding now on his initial summary from verses 1–2. He draws on various images and expressions to communicate his desire for divine forgiveness. He is clearly concerned with the sin itself, pleading with God to remove his sin (cleanse, wash), to hide his face from his sin, and to cover his sin (blot out). But although aware of the need for negative action to deal with the sin, the psalmist also desires a positive replacement, that is, the creation of something new within: "a pure heart . . . a steadfast spirit . . . the joy of your salvation . . . a willing spirit." At the heart of this positive replacement, however, is the psalmist's desire to remain in covenant relationship with God, typified by privileged access to his presence and the endowment of the Holy Spirit (see ch. 3, "David and Anointing").

The final part of this psalm clarifies the results that will flow when God fulfills the psalmist's requests of verses 7–12. The impact on the community as a whole is evident, for the psalmist will teach sinners to turn back to God

(v. 13), declare the praise of God (vv. 14–17), and renew proper worship among his people (vv. 18–19). The psalmist places his sin and repentance into the broader context of the community and shows the effect that repentance can have on an entire community of faith.

IMPLICATIONS

These three passages, 1 Samuel 11–12, 1 Samuel 24, and Psalm 51 with their depiction of David's sin and its consequences, reveal to us the human side of this king. The fact that the writer of Samuel chose to include these darker hues in the portrait of David suggests that there is no agenda of hero worship as one might expect. Instead, through these darker hues we become convinced of the need for a future royal figure in his line who would transcend the failings of not only David but also those who ruled in his place until the fall of Jerusalem in 587 B.C. Ultimately such a figure was identified by the church exclusively in the Davidic scion Jesus Christ who lived a blameless life, and through this Messiah the words of God through Nathan take on new significance for all those who believe on his name: "The LORD has taken away your sin. You are not going to die."

As we see David's struggle with sin, however, we also see the kind of struggle we all face. David's sin was not just a private affair, but rather impacted his family, Uriah's family, and ultimately the entire nation. This reminds us of the severe implications of sin for ourselves and for our communities of influence (e.g., family, church, business, land). But this event also reminds us that there is a way forward, that where sin abounds, grace abounds yet more. David's penitential response ("I have sinned against the LORD") is based on his confidence in the grace that God affords those who have broken his will. Receiving such grace, however, does demand penitential response, an admission of one's culpability before the Lord. David's struggle with sin also reminds us that although there are forgiveness and life, this does not eradicate the consequences of our sin. Although God spares David's life, he does not withdraw the promised discipline on his family. This warns us of the folly of "go[ing] on sinning so that grace may increase" (Rom 6:1).

David's mediatorial role in 1 Samuel 24 reminds us that ultimately Jesus would come as the perfect priestly-king in the order of Melchizedek (Heb. 7:17) who would transcend the temple built upon the threshing floor of Araunah the Jebusite. As Messiah he would function as priestly-king (Heb. 4:14–5:10; 7:1–28), as temple (John 1:14; 2:19–22), and as the sacrifice (Heb. 9–10) itself; and his actions would secure the mercy of God once for all.

It is through this account of failure that the gospel of the Messiah is illuminated for us. It reminds us of how central Christ's sacrifice on the cross is to our faith, not only as the act which has secured us acceptance before God, but also as the act that opens the way for a life of holiness and purity. It is sin that made this sacrifice necessary, but it is this sacrifice that breaks the power of sin over our lives.

The penitential prayer in Psalm 51 cries out to God based on a clear picture of who God is in relationship to our sin as well as a clear picture of who we are in relationship to our sin, and both of these are essential in repentance. On the divine side, God is both merciful and just; he will not overlook sin but invites us to him to find forgiveness. On the human side, we are sinful in action and disposition. In light of this, we are guided in confession in this psalm to ask God to deal with our sin in order that we might have restitution in our relationship with God, but also to renew within us a new spirit. This shows us that God's desire is deep transformation, rather than surface alterations. Such a vision is closely related to the New Testament teaching of sanctification, the deep work of God's Spirit to transform us into the image of Christ.

This psalm and the narratives of David's sin in Samuel challenge us to take seriously the impact of sin and penitence on the broader community. David's example has shown how the impact of sin is never limited to one individual. In the wake of his foolish act two families were destroyed, a nation was divided and disciplined. Nevertheless, there where sin increases, grace increases even more, and we see the truth of this in the impact of his penitence on the community as a whole: turning people back to God, declaring the mercy of God, and renewing the worship of God.

FOR FURTHER REFLECTION

1. As you have read through the account of David's sin, you may have been convicted by unresolved sin in your life from the past. Consider how you may resolve this issue, even if this means speaking privately with the one you have offended or paying restitution to those you have defrauded.

2. David's sin with Bathsheba highlights the importance of remaining faithful to God and avoiding sin. One enduring practice throughout the history of the church and evident throughout the Old Testament is confessing our sin to God. Such a practice not only keeps us from allowing sin to rule our lives, but it places us in a posture of grace in which we ask for the fullness of God's Spirit in order to walk in step with the Spirit. If this is not a regular component in your practice of spiritual disciplines individually and/or corporately, then take an opportunity to speak with God about those besetting sins

that threaten your spiritual vitality and could lead to severe consequences.

3. Nathan functioned as a court prophet, that is, a prophetic figure who functioned within the royal court and through whom God spoke to the king. As we see in this chapter, this prophetic voice was key to the spiritual vitality of David as king. Who is the Nathan in your life? To whom have you given the right to speak truth into your life? If there is no one, then begin to build a depth of friendship with another person who can speak into your life.

4. Second Samuel 24 points to David's role as mediator who secures forgiveness for the people, even at the expense of his own prosperity and life. As this value is ultimately expressed in and through Jesus, take a moment to celebrate his mediation for you and for those who believe.

5. In this passage we see the impact of a leader's failure on the people as a whole. David's sin had ramifications for more than just himself and his family, but rather endangered the nation. Meditate on this truth as a warning from the past (1 Cor. 10:1–13) and reflect on the ways your present patterns of living may be endangering the people in your sphere of influence.

6. We learn in this chapter that "the heart of David struck him," reminding us of the necessity of developing a good conscience. This means not ignoring or justifying sin when our conscience, informed and developed by regular study of the Word of God and communion with the people of God, signals that we are offending God's standards. Identify cases in the recent past when you have felt the tug of your conscience and yet have ignored it. Talk to God about this issue in your life.

7. Read through Psalm 139 and ask God to reveal to you any sin in your life. Reflect through the Ten Commandments (Ex. 20) and the Sermon on the Mount (Matt. 5–7), asking the Holy Spirit to reveal any issues, possibly praying: "Search me, O God, and know my heart; test me and know my anxious thoughts. See if there is any offensive way in me, and lead me in the way everlasting" (Ps. 139:23–24).

8. Reflect on God's mercy expressed through Jesus on the cross and extended to you by grace through faith in his name. Ask God for both cleansing of your sin and a renewal of faithfulness by the work of the Holy Spirit. Meditate through Psalm 51 as a prompt for confessing your sin to God.

9. Finally, in light of the conviction of Psalm 51 that repentance leads to teaching transgressors God's ways and turning sinners back to God, reflect on the ways that your repentance can bring a blessing to the community as a whole. Share your experience with another believer or even in a larger group setting as a testimony to God's grace.

13

DAVID AND MESSIAH

My earliest remembrance of the interpretation of the Old Testament in general, and of David and his dynasty in particular, is forever linked with cold Canadian winters and a child's expectation of Christmas. While most of the preaching that I heard was based either on a contemporary topic, a biblical theme, or a New Testament passage, once a year we knew there would be a sermon on the Old Testament in the Advent season. I knew the sermon genre well. The preacher would begin either with Genesis 3 ("he will crush your head, and you will strike his heel") or with Isaiah 7 ("Immanuel") and move through to the closing hope of Malachi 4 ("the prophet Elijah") as he traced the messianic hope that presaged the arrival of Jesus at the fullness of time. In many ways I am grateful for this regular rhythm during my childhood for it instilled in me an appreciation for the grand story of redemption that was as essential for ancient Jewish communities as it was for my own faith community (see Deut. 6, 26; Josh. 24; Pss. 104–106; Neh. 9). This tradition of tracing the signs of a coming ideal leadership figure is one deeply rooted in the experience of Israel. Although the tradition clearly preceded the Judean crisis and exile of the early sixth century B.C., there is no question that this event heightened such reflection to a new level.

PSALM 89: THE HISTORICAL AND
THEOLOGICAL CRISIS OF EXILE

One can understand the difficulty of the exilic period for those who took seriously the promises associated with the Davidic covenant. God had promised David an eternal dynasty enthroned at Jerusalem, the place of God's manifest presence. But in the early sixth century B.C. in several waves the great city was defeated, its structures destroyed, its people killed, exiled, or abused, and its monarchy removed and imprisoned, all signs of the removal of God's favor from the dynasty and city.

The struggle of those who clung to these ancient promises can be discerned clearly in Psalm 89.[1] The psalm begins on a positive and triumphant note as the psalmist expresses his intention to sing of the Lord's great love and faithfulness which stand firm forever (89:1-2). It is clear by verses 3-4 that a key theme of this psalm will be the Davidic covenant, even if at the outset no trouble can be discerned. The incomparability of the Lord for his covenant love and faithfulness is celebrated in verses 5-14 at the end of which the focus is on the Lord's kingship. In the following section (vv. 15-18), the psalmist returns to the theme of the human king, showing how the sign of God's blessing on his faithful subjects is the exaltation of their horn and shield (images of offensive and defensive protection), that is, their king.

These initial sections provide a strong foundation for the focus on the Davidic dynasty in the bulk of the psalm. The promise of God toward David is recited in careful detail in 89:19-37. Even though the psalmist accurately expresses the conditional character of each generation's participation in the Davidic covenantal blessings (vv. 30-32), it is also clear that such disobedience could never threaten the enduring promise of a line for David (vv. 33-37).

The tone of the psalm, however, shifts radically in verse 38 ("but you"), opening up a torrent of description of the recent catastrophes that had threatened the continuance of the Davidic line. The psalmist, who appears to be a Davidic descendant (vv. 47, 50), even accuses God of renouncing the covenant, while crying out for God to mercifully remember him in the midst of his crisis.

> O Lord, where is your former great love,
>> which in your faithfulness you swore to David?
> Remember, Lord, how your servant has been
>> mocked,
>> how I bear in my heart the taunts of all the
>> nations,
> the taunts with which your enemies have mocked,
>> O LORD,
> with which they have mocked every step of your
>> anointed one. (Ps. 89:49–51)

Although this psalm expresses legitimate concern over the covenant, crying to God to remember the promises expressed in 2 Samuel 7, it is well known from the book of Kings, however, that there were reasons for God's discipline of the Davidic kingdom. This is demonstrated clearly in passages like 2 Kings 23–25 (cf. 2 Kings 17) which trace the moral crisis of the Davidic house in the closing moments in the life of their kingdom (2 Kings 23:32, 37; 24:9, 19–20). It is this moral crisis that led to a crisis in the stability of Davidic kingship as king after king was removed from the throne by foreign leaders. However, in all of this the writer of Kings offers a glimmer of hope. In the closing paragraph of the book (2 Kings 25:27–30) the writer includes the story of the release of Jehoiachin from prison and the elevation of his status under the short rule of Nebuchadnezzar's son Amel-Marduk (Hebrew: Evil-Merodach). When Babylon was excavated in the nineteenth century, remains of the records of provisions provided to Jehoiachin and his sons were found in the palace area, testimony to the reality of this hope during the Babylonian exile.[2]

The Davidic house endured through the exile, and the Chronicler carefully records the generations of this line (1 Chron. 3). Biblical books from the early Persian period attest to the ascendancy of the Davidic line in the Persian provincial system in the person of Zerubbabel, grandson of Jehoiachin (Ezra 2–6; Hag. 1–2; Zech. 1–8), and the archaeological record contains reference to the co-rule of his daughter Shelomith with her husband Elnathan.[3]

Therefore, there is evidence of an enduring line of David in the dark period that precedes and follows the destruction of Jerusalem. It is in this period that an important witness matures in Israel, that is, the witness of the prophets. This witness begins the revelatory process of shaping an image of the future ideal Davidic king, often referred to as "Messiah," a term that was closely associated with the royal line.[4] The use of this term to close off the cry of Psalm 89 (v. 51) is witness to the need for this prophetic witness to sustain Israel through the period between the fall of Jerusalem and the arrival of Jesus.[5]

ISAIAH

Isaiah 1–39 and the Royal House

The focus of the first part of the book of Isaiah is clearly on the royal stream. Isaiah 6 provides an orientation to this section of the book with its contrast between the dying human Davidic king (Uzziah) and the enduring divine king (Yahweh). This prophetic call passage reveals an agenda of purification during the ministry of Isaiah that would not cease with the production of a remnant of a tenth (6:13a), but only with the creation of a "holy seed" (6:13b).

This introductory call prepares the way for chapters 7–39 which are structured around the response of two kings, Ahaz and Hezekiah, to the intimidation of the nations. The prophet encourages both kings to trust Yahweh to rescue the nation from these foreign powers (chs. 7–12, 36–38).[6] What lies between these two sections (both of which intertwine narrative and prophecy) is a series of prophetic pericopes focused on the nations. The purpose of this central section (chs. 13–35) is to reveal the folly of relying on the nations rather than Yahweh, a reliance to which Ahaz capitulates in chapters 7–12, but which Hezekiah ultimately resists in chapters 36–38. In light of the royal theme in this first phase of the book of Isaiah, it is not then surprising that many have noted that this section contains the greatest concentration of hope for a coming royal figure.

The starting point for most studies of this royal hope is Isaiah's confrontation of Ahaz in chapter 7 which results in the famous "Immanuel" prophecy. This prophecy announces the birth of a son who will presage the destruction of Ahaz's two enemies: Ephraim (Israel) and Aram. The birth of this child is called a "sign" from Yahweh. Interestingly, the prophecy associated with the Immanuel child of Isaiah 7 is reminiscent of that associated with a child who is born in chapter 8:

> The virgin will be with child and will give birth to a son, and will call him Immanuel. He will eat curds and honey when he knows enough to reject the wrong and choose the right. But before the boy knows enough to reject the wrong and choose the right, the land of the two kings you dread will be laid waste. (7:14–15)

> Then I went to the prophetess, and she conceived and gave birth to a son. And the LORD said to me,

"Name him Maher-Shalal-Hash-Baz. Before the boy knows how to say 'My father' or 'My mother,' the wealth of Damascus and the plunder of Samaria will be carried off by the king of Assyria." (8:3–4)

The link on the conceptual level is obvious: a woman giving birth to a child who is given a name and whose intellectual development marks the destruction of the foreign powers presently intimidating Ahaz. These conceptual links are bolstered by the use of identical vocabulary at several points: "give birth . . . son" (*yaladh* + *ben*), "call his name" (*qara'* + *shemo*), "before the boy knows" (*ki beterem yedha' hanna'ar*). These links strongly suggest that the Immanuel child is none other than Isaiah's child, Maher-Shalal-Hash-Baz. This conclusion is strengthened by the fact that 8:18 identifies Isaiah and his children as "signs," identical to the role of the Immanuel child in 7:14.[7]

Accompanying the description of the birth of Maher-Shalal-Hash-Baz is an oracle from God that addresses the Immanuel figure directly. Isaiah 8:6–10 reveals that the coming Assyrian punishment of the two kingdoms (Aram, Israel) would ultimately have ramifications for Judah as the rushing floodwaters of Assyria would sweep on into Judah until it reached "up to the neck" and its wings would "cover the breadth of your land, O Immanuel." This scenario is an obvious foreshadowing of the coming crisis under Hezekiah, who would hole up in his final fortified city, the capital Jerusalem, after the Assyrian Sennacherib had overrun his entire land. The designation of the land as "*your* land, O Immanuel," identifies someone as the promised child. In the previous line the oracle appears to allude to the period of Hezekiah (who would be either the head on top of the neck or trapped in the head, that is, the city), and if so, this line would be addressed to someone who lived during the time of Hezekiah. However, the oracle is addressed to Isaiah from Yahweh in the context of the birth narrative with no suggestion that Ahaz was involved at all. This evidence further supports the conclusion that the Immanuel child is the son of the prophet, whose land would face an Assyrian attack.

The child's role is to engender trust in Yahweh against insurmountable odds, an issue that is addressed in 8:9–10, ending with an allusion to the name Immanuel a second time (8:10b). The child is to be a catalyst for the kind of trust that was demanded of Ahaz in 7:9 and ultimately fulfilled in Hezekiah in 37:16–20. The promise of the Immanuel child, therefore, is not a *royal* messianic prophecy, for it is not concerned with an ideal royal figure. Nevertheless, this promise of an Immanuel child will exert much influence on the formation of messianic hope in Israel. It is just not part of the "royal" messianic stream of this hope, but rather among the prophetic messianic stream.[8]

Nevertheless, Isaiah 1–39 does contain other oracles that presage a future *royal* messianic figure. Isaiah 9:1–7 reflects the period after the Assyrian subjugation of the Northern Kingdom prophesied in chapters 7–8 (cf. 9:1). It looks to a future day of hope for the northern kingdom, a hope that is intricately linked to the appearance of a child who will reign on David's throne. His rule will be typified by the characteristics of justice and righteousness. All of this will be accomplished by the "zeal of Yahweh Almighty" (9:7).

Another allusion to the future of the Davidic line is found in chapter 11. There the future progeny is referred to as a shoot (*hoter*) from the stump (*geza'*) of Jesse, a branch (*netser*) from the roots (*shoreshim*) of Jesse, and later simply as the root (*shoresh*) of Jesse (11:1, 10). This image set suggests continuity with the ancient Davidic line alongside a new phase of growth for the tree.[9] Again the theme of justice and righteousness is associated with this royal figure, but in addition there is emphasis on the role of the Spirit of the Lord (*ruah YHWH*) who provides the qualities of wisdom associated with the Davidic line through the Solomonic wisdom tradition. This Davidic progeny is also associated with universal peace in creation due to global knowledge of the Lord. The remnant of Israel (both Ephraim and Judah) will rally to this Davidic figure who will lead them in victory over their enemies.[10]

In the midst of an oracle against Moab in Isaiah 16:4–5, Isaiah prophesies the establishment of a throne upon which a man from the house of David would sit. This royal figure is typified again as one who not only "seeks justice," but also "speeds the cause of righteousness" (see ch. 7, "David and Justice").

The focus on Hezekiah and his faith in the midst of trying circumstances in chapters 36–38 suggests that he is the expected Davidic figure who is closely associated with the remnant (37:31–32) and the "zeal of Yahweh Almighty" (37:32b). However, Isaiah 1–39 is shaped in such a way as to indicate that Hezekiah does not fill out these prophecies fully. First, although Isaiah 6:13 does refer to a remnant of a tenth, it then declares that even that remnant would be laid waste to the point that all that would be left would be a seed. This matches the structure of Isaiah 7–39. Indeed, a remnant is left and is identified as Hezekiah and his generation, but this remnant would ultimately face an even greater destruction in the Babylonian period which is foreshadowed in the narrative of Isaiah 39. Second, Isaiah 39 highlights the ultimate folly of Hezekiah as one whose actions would seal the fate of Judah and the Davidic line. It is important to note that the judgment of Isaiah on Hezekiah in 39:5–7 is focused on the Davidic line both past and future ("all that your fathers have stored up until this day . . . your own flesh and blood who will be born to you"). The final shape of Isaiah 1–39 certainly affirms an enduring hope for the Davidic line, but does not limit such hope to Hezekiah.

Isaiah 1–39 places much hope on the Davidic line and focuses much attention on the bright figure of Hezekiah against the dark backdrop of his father Ahaz. This hope is ultimately transferred into the exilic future with the failure of Hezekiah.

Isaiah 40–66

While Isaiah 39 serves as an important conclusion to the first part of the book, it also shifts the attention to those who lived in the wake of the fulfillment of the ominous prediction of Isaiah. The focus of this part of Isaiah is on the revitalization of a community which has experienced the exile.

This community is referred to both as Jerusalem/Zion and Israel/Jacob, and it is in connection with the second range of titles (Israel/Jacob) that a stream of messianic expectation is often discerned. Israel and Jacob are identified in Isaiah 40–66 as "my servant(s)" (41:8–9; 42:19; 43:10; 44:1–2, 21; 45:4; 48:20; 49:3, 5–7; 52:13; 53:11; 65:9, 15).[11] The term "servant" is associated in the Old Testament with a variety of figures ranging from Moses to Joshua to David to the prophets to the Levites to the people as a whole. There is little question that the servant image here is associated with the people who have experienced the suffering of the exile as clearly demonstrated in the positive tone of 41:8–10; 43:10; 44:1–5, 21–23; 45:4; 48:20; 49:3, and the negative rebuke of 42:18–25.[12] However, at certain points this servant figure is identified as one who does something on behalf of Israel and Jacob, and it is this aspect of the servant motif in Isaiah 40–66 that has often been cited as evidence of a messianic figure.[13]

The first of this evidence can be discerned in Isaiah 49:1–9. At first it appears that the prophetic voice is acting the part of Israel as he describes Yahweh's call: "You are my servant, Israel, in whom I will display my splendor" (49:3). However, 49:5–9 reveals that this servant figure has a role to play in relationship to Israel and Jacob: "to bring Jacob back to him and gather Israel to himself . . . to restore the tribes of Jacob and bring back those of Israel I have kept . . . to be a covenant for the people, to restore the land and to reassign its desolate inheritances, to say to the captives, 'Come out,' and to those in darkness, 'Be free!'" Second, this same nuance can be discerned in the well-known passage 52:13–53:12 where the servant figure is described as one suffering vicariously on behalf of a corporate body (we, our, us). Third, another voice, often associated with the servant, emerges in 61:1–3, and again this voice makes promises to captives and prisoners and those who grieve in Zion.

Now it is possible that this could be a reference to a smaller remnant group which will play a role within the larger entity of "Israel/Jacob," but this seems to be pressing the evidence to the breaking point. Many have suggested that this servant figure is Cyrus, who is presented in Isaiah 44:24–45:13 as an "anointed" figure who serves the interests of Israel/Jacob. However, the role of Cyrus is limited to breaking the hegemony of Babylon over Israel/Jacob, releasing Israel/Jacob from exile, and rebuilding city and temple, and is never related to the vicarious suffering motif.

The language associated with this suffering servant figure appears to be connected more to a prophetic rather than a royal role in ancient Israel. Isaiah 49:1–6 speaks of a "mouth like a sharpened sword" and a commissioning to bring back Jacob and Israel and to be a light to the Gentiles. A figure speaks in 50:4–10 and this one celebrates the fact that God has given him "an instructed tongue, to know the word that sustains the weary" (v. 4). Again a voice breaks forth in 61:1–3, and this voice speaks of the Spirit upon him "to preach good news to the poor . . . to proclaim freedom for the captives." These examples suggest a ministry of speaking rather than ruling.

The suffering servant figure is a prophetic figure who will act on behalf of Israel, proclaiming God's promise to them, announcing God's salvation of them, and experiencing God's punishment for them.

This does not mean, however, that there is no reference to a royal figure in Isaiah 40–66. The message of Isaiah 55 is clearly directed to the community as a whole who are invited to seek the Lord through entering into covenant with him. In connection with this covenant, Yahweh reminds them of the covenant that he made with David, a covenant that secured an international role for the royal house. Some have seen this as evidence of a democratization of the Davidic covenant, that is, the transferal of the Davidic covenant from the royal house to the community as a whole. However, it is also possible that the prophet is arguing that the covenant to which Yahweh is inviting the people is based upon the enduring covenant that God has made with the royal house. Thus as with the servant and Israel/Jacob, an individual from within the group has a key role to play for the entire community. In this case, there is enduring hope for the Davidic line.

JEREMIAH

Jeremiah's message is extremely harsh against the leaders of his day. There will be no mercy for royal, priestly, and prophetic figures as well as the people of Jerusalem, all of whom will drink the cup of God's wrath (13:12–14) and have their bones exposed to the heavenly bodies they worship (8:1–3). No leadership group is spared Jeremiah's criticism, but one should not miss the strong message against the royal line. In 36:30–31, following Jehoiakim's calloused burning of Jeremiah's scroll, Jeremiah prophesies that the king's body will be thrown out and exposed, his children punished, and that no one will sit on the throne of David for him. A similar tone is directed at his son Jehoiachin, who is rejected as God's signet ring in Jeremiah 22.

In the midst of this harsh critique and dire warning, however, there is evidence of a future hope. Immediately following the rejection of Jehoiachin (22:24–30) and the subsequent woe oracle against the destructive shepherds (23:1–2), God promises to shepherd the people and place over them good shepherds. These shepherds are identified through the redactional insertion of 23:5–6 with the raising up of a Davidic figure who is called Zemah (often translated "Branch") and to whom is attributed the qualities of righteous rule.

Such a promise is not completely out of place in the book of Jeremiah. It is foreshadowed in 3:15 with God's promise that he will give the people shepherds after his own heart when they return to the land. It is suggested in 17:25 as an enticement for obedience to Sabbath law: "then kings who sit on David's throne will come through the gates of the city with their officials." It is mentioned in passing in the promise of a restoration from exile to "serve the LORD their God and David their king whom I will raise up for them" (30:8–9).

This expectation for a coming royal figure named Zemah is repeated in 33:15–16, but with a slight twist. Now linked to this royal figure is a second figure, a priestly figure who will stand before Yahweh and offer sacrifices (33:17–26).[14] Future expectation is now broadened to include royal and priestly streams.

The final chapters of the book of Jeremiah provide a surprise for readers, especially in light of the strong rebuke and rejection of Jehoiachin in chapter 22. In contrast, Jeremiah 52:31–34 rehearses Jehoiachin's release from prison, suggesting that those responsible for the book of Jeremiah as a whole celebrated this release as a sign of hope for the future of Judah. It is difficult to avoid the conclusion that such hope was also attached to the Davidic line to which

Jehoiachin belonged. The inclusion of the Jehoiachin release would be in line with the enduring royal hope demonstrated elsewhere in this book.

The Jeremianic tradition thus places great emphasis on a future royal figure who will rule with justice, but at some point also creates space for a future priestly figure whose fortunes are intimately linked with royal expectation.

EZEKIEL

Expectations for future ideal figures in Ezekiel 1–39 are restricted to the royal stream. At two points (Ezekiel 34:23–24; 37:24–28) hope is expressed for a shepherd alongside the Lord who is called "my servant David." In both passages he is referred to as "prince" (*nasi'*), but in the second also as "king" (*melek*). This first term (*nasi'*) plays an important royal role in Ezekiel 40–48, the section of the prophetic book that offers a vision of a restored temple, worship, and community. There a figure called "prince" (*nasi'*; Ezek. 44:3 [2x]; 45:7, 16, 17, 22; 46:2, 4, 8, 10, 12, 16, 17, 18; 48:21 [2x], 22 [2x]) plays a role within the restoration that is spearheaded by priests who are Levites and descendants of Zadok (Ezek. 40:46; 43:19; 44:15; 48:11) who contrast with Levites who "went far away."

This prince is clearly associated with royal figures who had previously abused the people through social injustice (45:8–12). In spite of this, the prince is given access to the sanctuary where he will eat bread before Yahweh (44:3). He is also given a special allotment of land close to the holy site (45:7). The prince is responsible to provide the various offerings in order to "make atonement for the house of Israel" (45:17).

The book of Ezekiel, therefore, includes a future royal hope alongside its priestly vision, identifying the royal stream with the future renewal of the Davidic line and the priestly with the future renewal of the Zadokite line.

HOSEA, AMOS, MICAH

Hosea, Amos, and Micah all express great displeasure with royal figures of their day (Hos. 1:1, 4; 5:1–2; 8:4; 10:3–4; 13:9–11; Amos 1:1, 15; 7:9, 13; Mic. 1:1, 14; 3:1, 11; 6:16), alongside an expectation for a future royal figure. Hosea 2:2 (Eng. 1:11) makes passing mention of a future leader (*ro'sh 'ehadh*, "one head") who will be appointed by the reunited and restored tribes of Israel. The character of this leader is made explicit in Hosea 3:4–5, which also looks to the restoration of the community after exile. When they return to the land, the Israelites will seek "the LORD their God and David their king."

The book of Amos also associates future restoration with the Davidic line through the promise of the restoration of "David's fallen tent" (9:11–12). In this case, however, it is difficult to know whether this is a metaphor for the restoration of Davidic rule or restoration of the city of Jerusalem, especially in light of the promise to "repair its broken places, restore its ruins, and build it as it used to be." The latter seems more probable.

Finally, the book of Micah sends mixed messages on the future of kingship. In the context of imminent defeat for the royal house (5:1), it remains fixated on a future reestablishment of Davidic kingship with its prophecy of a ruler coming forth from Bethlehem with ancient pedigree who will stand and shepherd his flock (5:2–5a). This figure will do so in God's strength, bearing God's majesty and providing security and peace by extending his authority to the "ends of the earth." At the same time, however, there is also an emphasis in Micah on divine kingship. In 2:12–13 God promises to gather the remnant of Israel and as "their king . . . pass through before them . . . at their head." Similarly, in 4:6–8 God promises to gather the exiles and rule from Mount Zion. The kingship that is restored appears to be the kingship of the Lord in Zion.

HAGGAI, ZECHARIAH

Both Haggai and Zechariah, who prophesy under Persian rule in the early phase of the restoration from Babylonian exile, see in their present day the beginning of fulfillment of aspects of the earlier prophetic messianic hope. Both of these prophets address two key figures who were instrumental during the reign of Darius: Zerubbabel and Jeshua (Hag. 1:1, 12–14; 2:1–4, 20–23; Zech. 3:1–10; 4:6–10; 6:9–15). Zerubbabel was the grandson of Jehoiachin, the second last king of Judah, whose release from prison is recorded at the end of 2 Kings and Jeremiah. Jeshua was the grandson of Seraiah, the final high priest of Judah, whose death at the hands of the Babylonians marks the end of worship at the first temple sponsored by the Davidic dynasty (2 Kings 25:18–21).

Although Haggai's mention of both Zerubbabel and Jeshua reveals attention to the royal and priestly lines associated with the line of David, it is Zerubbabel who receives the greater attention. In the closing prophecy of the book, Haggai anticipates a day when the Davidic dynasty will realize the universal hegemony associated with it throughout the Old Testament witness (Hag. 2:20–23). Using language associated with the appointment of Davidic kings ("take . . . my servant . . . make you . . . chosen"), the prophet reveals that the earlier judgment of Jeremiah against Jehoiachin as the Lord's signet ring (Jer. 22) will come to an end "on that day" as God restores the Davidic line and propels its representative to the place of vice-regent over all creation. Zerubbabel is the focus of this promise, but stands as representative of the Davidic line.

Zechariah also echoes the fulfillment of Jeremiah's future hope. He looks to the emergence of the Zemah figure that was so integral to Jeremiah's royal vision and sees in the reestablishment of priestly service in Jeshua the first signs of the reemergence of the Davidic dynasty in Zerubbabel (Zech. 3:1–10; 4:6–10; 6:9–15). Accompanying this reemergence will be the rebuilt temple and a new day of prosperity for the people of God.

Zechariah 7–8, however, reveals that there are enduring problems within the Jewish community in this restoration period, patterns of spiritual and social dysfunction that will stifle the renewal. The latter half of the book of Zechariah does keep alive the royal hope with its celebration of a royal Davidic figure in 9:9–10, a king of Jerusalem associated with the promise to Judah who will ride into his reclaimed capital on a donkey. The rest of Zechariah 9–14 expresses enduring hope for the line of David, even if it must be cleansed (12:8, 10, 12; 13:1). In the final chapter (14:9), however, the Lord himself is identified as the king, revealing the primacy of the Lord for the future of the Davidic line.

JESUS CHRIST

This long line of prophetic witnesses highlights an enduring hope for the Davidic royal line. As discussed in our initial chapter, the New Testament writers clearly identified Jesus as this royal Messiah, in whom all these hopes for David's line had now come to fulfillment. God's promise expressed through Jacob in his blessing of Judah in Genesis 49 which was formalized in God's covenant ceremony with David in 2 Samuel 7 would only finally reach fulfillment in all its dimensions in and through Jesus. These prophetic passages which nurtured the hope of Israel throughout the challenges of life after the crises of the sixth century B.C. were essential to the early church. Links established between this prophetic witness and the ministry of Jesus were important to earlier Christian theological reflection and apologetic witness. In this way, the prophetic witness nurtured the faith of the church as they traced the ways in which God's promises were fulfilled in Jesus. Furthermore, the prophetic witness was a guide to those aspects of the messianic hope that were still to be fulfilled in the second advent of Jesus. For those of us living in the third millennium since that first advent, these texts encourage our faith in our Messiah even as they remind us of the many qualities of David that were fulfilled climactically and perfectly in Jesus. As the messianic community longing for the return of Messiah Jesus, the son of David, we are not only encouraged by these prophetic texts, but challenged to live as Christ-ones, reflecting the values we have discovered throughout this book.

FOR FURTHER REFLECTION

1. Although as Christians we now live in the light of the coming of Messiah Jesus, we still share much in common with those who heard these prophets of old. As they awaited the coming of their royal messiah, so we await the second coming of Messiah Jesus. The prophetic witness which looked to Jesus thus grants us confidence that as God fulfilled his promise to bring a Messiah, so he will fulfill his promise to return again. Express your praise to God as the one who fulfills his promises and your trust in his promises for the future.

2. Take this opportunity at the end of the book to reflect back over the many themes we have considered in

our study of the figure of David in the Old Testament: Anointing, Covenant, Rule, Faith, Justice, Unity, Worship, Temple, Faithfulness, and Sin. Identify which of these values were most significant for your spiritual development and share this with another person within the next day.

FOR FURTHER READING

Allender, Dan B., and Tremper Longman. *The Cry of the Soul: How Our Emotions Reveal Our Deepest Questions About God.* Colorado Springs: NavPress, 1994.

Arnold, Bill T. *1–2 Samuel.* Grand Rapids: Zondervan, 2003.

Bar-Efrat, Shimeon. *Narrative Art in the Bible.* Journal for the Study of the Old Testament, Supplement 70. Sheffield: Almond Press, 1989.

Boda, Mark J. "Figuring the Future: The Prophets and the Messiah." In *Messiah*, edited by Stanley E. Porter. McMaster New Testament Studies. Grand Rapids: Eerdmans, 2007.

———. *Haggai/Zechariah.* Grand Rapids: Zondervan, 2004.

Brown, Raymond E. *The Birth of the Messiah: A Commentary on the Infancy Narratives in the Gospels of Matthew and Luke.* Updated ed. Anchor Bible Reference Library. New York: Doubleday, 1993.

Brueggemann, Walter. "The Costly Loss of Lament." *Journal for the Study of the Old Testament* 36 (1986): 57–71.

———. *The Message of the Psalms: A Theological Commentary.* Augsburg Old Testament Studies. Minneapolis: Augsburg, 1984.

Brueggemann, Walter, and Patrick D. Miller. *The Psalms and the Life of Faith.* Minneapolis: Fortress, 1995.

Craigie, Peter C. *Psalms 1–50.* Word Biblical Commentary 19. Waco, TX.: Word Books, 1983.

Davies, Philip R. *In Search of "Ancient Israel."* Journal for the Study of the Old Testament, Supplement 148. Sheffield: Sheffield Academic, 1992.

Davies, W. D., and Dale C. Allison. *A Critical and Exegetical Commentary on the Gospel According to Matthew*. International Critical Commentary. Edinburgh: T. & T. Clark, 1988.

Dever, William G. "Archaeology, Urbanism and the Rise of the Israelite State." In *Urbanism in Antiquity: From Mesopotamia to Crete*, edited by Walter E. Aufrecht, Neil A. Mirau, and Steven W. Gauley, 172–93. Journal for the Study of the Old Testament, Supplement 244. Sheffield: JSOT Press, 1997.

DeVries, Simon J. "Moses and David as Cult Founders in Chronicles." *Journal of Biblical Literature* 107 (1988): 619–39.

Fisch, Harold. "Ruth and the Structure of Covenant History." *Vetus Testamentum* 32.4 (1982): 425–37.

Flanagan, James W. *David's Social Drama: A Hologram of Israel's Early Iron Age*. Journal for the Study of the Old Testament, Supplement 73. Sheffield: Sheffield Academic, 1988.

Gerbrandt, Gerald Eddie. *Kingship According to the Deuteronomistic History*. Atlanta: Scholars, 1986.

Halpern, Baruch. *David's Secret Demons: Messiah, Murderer, Traitor, King*. Grand Rapids: Eerdmans, 2001.

Howard, David M. "The Transfer of Power from Saul to David in 1 Sam 16:13–14." *Journal of the Evangelical Theological Society* 32.4 (1989): 473–83.

Isser, Stanley. *The Sword of Goliath: David in Heroic Literature*. Studies in Biblical Literature. Atlanta: Society of Biblical Literature, 2004.

Kaminsky, Joel S. *Corporate Responsibility in the Hebrew Bible*. Journal for the Study of the Old Testament, Supplement 196. Sheffield: Sheffield Academic, 1995.

Knoppers, Gary N. "Ancient Near Eastern Royal Grants and the Davidic Covenant: A Parallel?" *Journal of the American Oriental Society* 116.4 Oct–Dec (1996): 670–97.

Kraus, Hans-Joachim. *Psalms 1–59: A Commentary*. Continental Commentaries. Minneapolis: Augsburg, 1988.

Mays, James Luther. *The Lord Reigns: A Theological Handbook to the Psalms*. Interpretation, a Bible Commentary for Teaching and Preaching. Louisville, KY.: Westminster John Knox, 1994.

McKenzie, Steven L. *King David: A Biography*. Oxford: Oxford University Press, 2000.

Piper, John. *Let the Nations Be Glad: The Supremacy of God in Missions*. Grand Rapids: Baker, 1993.

———. *The Supremacy of God in Preaching*. Grand Rapids: Baker, 1990.

Provan, Iain, V. Phillips Long, and Tremper Longman III. *A Biblical History of Israel*. Louisville: Westminster John Knox, 2003.

Rost, Leonhard. *The Succession to the Throne of David*. Historic Texts and Interpreters in Biblical Scholarship 1. Sheffield: Almond, 1982.

Ryken, Leland, and Tremper Longman III. *A Complete Literary Guide to the Bible*. Grand Rapids: Zondervan, 1993.

Schaberg, J. *The Illegitimacy of Jesus*. New York: Crossroad, 1990.

Thompson, Thomas L. *Early History of the Israelite People: From the Written and Archaeological Sources*. Studies in the History of the Ancient Near East 4. Leiden: Brill, 1992.

Van Seters, John. *In Search of History: Historiography in the Ancient World and the Origins of Biblical History*. New Haven: Yale University Press, 1983.

———. *Prologue to History: The Yahwist as Historian in Genesis*. Louisville, KY: Westminster John Knox, 1992.

Weinfeld, M. "The Covenant of Grant in the Old Testament and in the Ancient Near East." *Journal of the American Oriental Society* 90.2 (1970): 184–203.

Westermann, Claus. *Praise and Lament in the Psalms*. Atlanta: John Knox, 1981.

Williamson, H. G. M. *Variations on a Theme: King, Messiah, and Servant in the Book of Isaiah*. Carlisle: Paternoster, 1998.

NOTES

CHAPTER ONE: DAVID AND BIBLICAL THEOLOGY

1   Other extrabiblical references to David have also been identified in
    the Mesha Inscription (sometimes called the Moabite Stone) from
    mid-ninth century B.C. and in a list by Pharaoh Shoshenq I (late
    tenth century B.C.). See further, I. Provan, V. P. Long, and T. Long-
    man III, *A Biblical History of Israel* (Louisville: Westminster John
    Knox, 2003), 194.

2   J. Van Seters, *In Search of History: Historiography in the Ancient
    World and the Origins of Biblical History* (New Haven: Yale Uni-
    versity Press, 1983); J. W. Flanagan, *David's Social Drama: A Holo-
    gram of Israel's Early Iron Age* (JSOTSup 73; Sheffield: Sheffield
    Academic, 1988); J. Van Seters, *Prologue to History: The Yahwist as
    Historian in Genesis* (Louisville: Westminster John Knox, 1992);
    T. L. Thompson, *Early History of the Israelite People: From the Writ-
    ten and Archaeological Sources* (SHANE 4; Leiden: Brill, 1992);
    P. R. Davies, *In Search of "Ancient Israel"* (JSOTSup 148; Sheffield:
    Sheffield Academic, 1992).

3   See responses by W. G. Dever, "Archaeology, Urbanism and the Rise
    of the Israelite State," in *Urbanism in Antiquity: From Mesopotamia
    to Crete*, ed. W. E. Aufrecht, N. A. Mirau, and S. W. Gauley (JSOT-
    Sup 244; Sheffield: JSOT Press, 1997), 172–93; B. Halpern, *David's
    Secret Demons: Messiah, Murderer, Traitor, King* (Grand Rapids:
    Eerdmans, 2001).

4   The distinction here is based on Christ's statements on divorce
    in Matthew 19. There Jesus claims that the Mosaic law "permit-
    ted" divorce, but that "it was not this way from the beginning"

(v. 8) One can distinguish then between God's permissive will and his initiatory will.

5   It is not Barak who is identified as a judge in Judges 4–5, but rather Deborah.

6   It has often been noted that there are two introductions to the book of Judges (1:1–2:5 and 2:6–3:6). The second is clearly related to the "judges" cycles, setting up the basic framework for these narratives. The first introduction, however, with its focus on tribal identity and echo of the battle inquiry found in 20:18, is related to chapters 17–21.

CHAPTER TWO: DAVID, ABRAHAM, AND RUTH

1   In Genesis 26:34–35, we are told that Esau marries two Hittite women; in Genesis 38, Judah marries a Canaanite woman. These Canaanite peoples were marked for judgment by God. Intermarrying with them would include Abraham's seed in their judgment. In the case of Genesis 38, Joseph is clearly raised up to rescue the rest of his family from such danger, providing a temporary land where they may grow into a nation clearly delineated from its surrounding culture, since the Egyptians detested shepherds (Gen. 46:34).

2   In ancient patriarchal societies, it was proper for the widow to return to the house of her father after the death of her husband. She would not remain within the house of her husband. Orpah's behavior is in keeping with ancient traditions (Ruth 1:14).

3   There is some ambiguity in the book of Ruth on this law, since it is Naomi and Ruth who are selling the property to the kinsman-redeemer, whereas in the Torah, the land is sold to a non-kinsman-redeemer and the kinsman-redeemer then redeems the land from the third party.

4   Ruth's behavior is forward and suggests to many a sexual advance (Ruth 3:9), the danger of which is recognized by Boaz's careful instructions to her (3:11–14); for this see especially R. E. Brown, *The Birth of the Messiah: A Commentary on the Infancy Narratives in the Gospels of Matthew and Luke*, updated ed. (Anchor Bible Reference Library; New York: Doubleday, 1993), 71–74; W. D. Davies and D. C. Allison, *A Critical and Exegetical Commentary on*

the Gospel According to Matthew (ICC; Edinburgh: T. & T. Clark, 1988), 1:169–72; J. Schaberg, *The Illegitimacy of Jesus* (New York: Crossroad, 1990).

5 Rahab and Tamar were Canaanites, Ruth was a Moabitess. Although Bathsheba was Jewish, notice how she is called "the wife of Uriah" (who was a Hittite, 2 Sam. 11:3) in the genealogy of Jesus (Matt. 1:6).

6 See further H. Fisch, "Ruth and the Structure of Covenant History," *VT* 32.4 (1982): 425–37.

CHAPTER THREE: DAVID AND ANOINTING

1 D. M. Howard, "The Transfer of Power from Saul to David in 1 Sam 16:13–14," *JETS* 32 (1989): 473–83. The concern that God not take his Holy Spirit from David in Psalm 51:11 is thus a concern over the loss of royal office, rather than over personal salvation.

2 See M. J. Boda, "Figuring the Future: The Prophets and the Messiah," in *Messiah*, ed. S. E. Porter (McMaster New Testament Studies; Grand Rapids: Eerdmans, 2007).

CHAPTER FOUR: DAVID AND COVENANT

1 Even though the word "covenant" (*berith*) never appears in 2 Samuel 7, other texts refer to this agreement as such: 2 Sam. 23:5; Ps. 89:3, 28, 34, 39.

2 Note the contrast that Weinfeld makes between two types of treaties in the ancient Near East, one typified by the suzerainty treaty (often linked to the Sinai covenant) and the other typified by the royal land grant (often linked to the Abrahamic and Davidic covenants); see M. Weinfeld, "The Covenant of Grant in the Old Testament and in the Ancient Near East," *JAOS* 90 (1970): 184–203. Although contrast G. N. Knoppers, "Ancient Near Eastern Royal Grants and the Davidic Covenant: A Parallel?" *JAOS* 116 (1996): 670–97.

3 While some may suggest that the term used here (*'anah*) refers to the intense effort of David to bring the ark to Jerusalem, it is used elsewhere to refer to severe affliction inflicted by another party (Isa. 53:4; Ps. 119:71) or to humbling oneself (Lev. 23:29).

4 A similar reciprocity can be seen in the confirmation of the Abrahamic covenant in Genesis 17 and the Sinai covenant in Deuteronomy 26:16–19.

5   A slight contrast is that 2 Samuel 7 speaks of an eternally guaran-
teed throne for David's descendants that may involve the discipline
of one generation, but not bring into jeopardy the continuance of
the line, whereas Psalm 132:12 speaks of the future of the line as
dependent on the obedience of each generation.

CHAPTER FIVE: DAVID AND RULE

1   This is apparent from the reaction of Athaliah who merely has to
see the activities taking place in 11:14 and knows what is going on.

2   J. L. Mays, *The Lord Reigns: A Theological Handbook to the Psalms*
(Interpretation; Louisville: Westminster John Knox, 1994), 110–11.
Although H.-J. Kraus does see this as a royal psalm, he stops short
of an enthronement festival (*Psalms 1–59* [Minneapolis: Augsburg,
1988], 126).

3   For the comparison between Egypt and Mesopotamia and the
view of adoption see Kraus, *Psalms 1–59*, 130–32. Kraus notes
that in the Code of Hammurabi when a father adopts children of
a female slave, he declares: "You are my children." So similarly
the Lord in Exodus 4:22 and Deuteronomy 14:1. Contra P. C.
Craigie, *Psalms 1–50* (WBC 19; Waco, Tex.: Word Books, 1983),
62–68, who seeks for a via media between adoption and conception, even though he maintains that the Davidic king was a
human being.

4   The word for son in the Hebrew text here is *bar* rather than *ben*,
as is found in 2:7. The word *bar* is the Aramaic word for son. Some
textual witnesses suggest the Hebrew *bor* (purity) or *bar* (clean,
pure) and there is a Ugaritic root *brr* (pure one, shining one); see
Kraus, *Psalms 1–59*, 130–32. Craigie, *Psalms 1–50*, 62–68, sees no
problem with the Aramaic "son" because it is an ancient language
and comes in a section addressed to foreign kings in what was a
key diplomatic language in the ancient Near East.

5   The prefix *Jeru* may mean "city/town of."

CHAPTER SIX: DAVID AND FAITH

1   The Chronicler uses the verb *darash* here in place of *sha'al*, but, first
of all, these terms are synonymous (cf. 1 Kings 22:5–8); second, the
verb *darash* is used in 1 Samuel 28:7 when referring to Saul's inquiry

of the medium at Endor and so influenced the Chronicler's terminology here; and third, *darash* is a favored term of the Chronicler.

CHAPTER SEVEN: DAVID AND JUSTICE

1 *Ancient Near Eastern Texts Relating to the Old Testament*, ed. James B. Pritchard (Princeton: Princeton University Press, 1955), 164.

2 It is uncertain whether the figures in Isaiah 42 and 61 can be securely linked to the Davidic dynasty (see ch. 13, "David and Messiah").

3 "Sea to sea" is unclear: this could be the Mediterranean and Dead Sea or Mediterranean and Red Sea, if the former then a west-east axis, if the latter then west-south extremities which are then matched by north-east extremities of "the River" (Euphrates) and "the ends of the earth." Tarshish and islands are western extremities, Sheba/Seba are southern or eastern. Probably here we have different extremities which function to establish an image of universality.

4 Psalm 72 is located at the "seam" between two books of the Psalter (Book II: Pss. 42–72 and Book III: Pss. 73–89). The final three verses (72:18–20) are not part of the psalm itself, but rather are part of the editorial framework of the book of Psalms, with verses 18–19 representing one of the doxologies that end each of the books (cf. Pss. 41:13; 89:52; 106:48; 145:21) and verse 20 comprising an editorial note of the end of an earlier collection of Davidic prayers. See M. J. Boda, "'Declare His Glory Among the Nations': The Psalter as Missional Collection," in *Christian Mission: Old Testament Foundations and New Testament Development*, ed. S. E. Porter and C. Long Westfall (Grand Rapids: Eerdmans, forthcoming).

CHAPTER EIGHT: DAVID AND UNITY

1 At points there are subtle allusions to the exilic experience: Pss. 120, 124, 126, 129, 132.

2 Psalm 120:5 has mystified some interpreters because the psalmist speaks of dwelling "in Meshech . . . among the tents of Kedar." Meshech is in Asia Minor to the far north while Kedar is in the Syro-Arabian desert to the east of Israel. Some have suggested that this is a merism for life at the fringes of civilization, but a closer look

at the verse reveals that he is dwelling *in* Meshech, while he is *among the tents* of Kedar. The Kedarites were Arabians well known for their role in ancient trade. The psalmist is thus a servant of the Kedarites who are trading in Meshech.

CHAPTER NINE: DAVID AND WORSHIP

1 S. J. De Vries, "Moses and David as Cult Founders in Chronicles," *JBL* 107 (1988): 619–39.

2 It is rather ironic that the one to whom the Spirit of God had gone from Saul is the one who is used to appease the injurious spirit God sent in the place of his Spirit resting on Saul (1 Sam. 16).

3 C. Westermann, *Praise and Lament in the Psalms* (Atlanta: John Knox, 1981).

4 W. Brueggemann, *The Message of the Psalms: A Theological Commentary* (Augsburg Old Testament Studies; Minneapolis: Augsburg, 1984); W. Brueggemann and P. D. Miller, *The Psalms and the Life of Faith* (Minneapolis: Fortress, 1995).

5 J. Piper, *Let the Nations Be Glad: The Supremacy of God in Missions* (Grand Rapids: Baker, 1993); J. Piper, *The Supremacy of God in Preaching* (Grand Rapids: Baker, 1990).

6 See further the excellent book of D. B. Allender and T. Longman III, *The Cry of the Soul: How Our Emotions Reveal Our Deepest Questions About God* (Colorado Springs: NavPress, 1994).

7 W. Brueggemann, "The Costly Loss of Lament," *JSOT* 36 (1986): 57–71.

CHAPTER TEN: DAVID AND TEMPLE

1 There is an allusion to renewed glory in Haggai 2:1–9, but this glory is a reference to the material glory of the second temple, although this may have been an expression of a faint hope for the return of God's glory. Zechariah attaches great hope to the renewal of the temple as well, but the enduring sinfulness of the people frustrates the final declaration of God's renewed presence. See M. J. Boda, *Haggai/Zechariah* (Grand Rapids: Zondervan, 2004), 126–26.

CHAPTER ELEVEN: DAVID AND FAITHFULNESS

1 A similar triangulation for effect can be discerned in the writer's introduction of Saul's daughter Michal, who like her brother

Jonathan sides with David against her father's wishes (1 Sam. 19:11–17).

2   In contrast to Baruch Halpern, who sees this as evidence that David became Jonathan's shield bearer (*David's Secret* [Grand Rapids: Eerdmans, 2001], 19).

3   Although see the extraordinary display of Jacob toward his cousin Rachel in Genesis 29:11.

4   It is ludicrous to see here a reference to homosexuality, especially in light of David's clear heterosexuality. The point is that the level of intimacy between these two men was extraordinary even beyond the intimacy they each shared with women. On this issue see further B. T. Arnold, *1–2 Samuel* (Grand Rapids: Zondervan, 2003), 271–73.

5   Probably the original form of the name was Mephibaal ("from the mouth of Baal"), but in the Hebrew text to avoid mention of the god Baal, the word *bosheth* ("shame") was inserted. The switch to Meribbaal may have been due to the similarity between the Hebrew consonants *resh* (*r*) and *pe* (*p*). See further D. V. Edelman, "Mephib-sheth," in *Anchor Bible Dictionary* (New York: Doubleday, 1992), 6:696–97.

6   It is uncertain which side of the story one should believe. Indeed, from David's decision to divide the land in two (half for Ziba and half for Mephibosheth), it appears that even he was not certain. In any case, David remained faithful to his covenant with Jonathan even after Mephibosheth's disloyalty, refusing to punish him when he had a splendid opportunity (2 Sam. 21:8–9).

CHAPTER TWELVE: DAVID AND SIN

1   So also Uriah's faithful behavior as soldier later in the chapter contrasts with David's unfaithful behavior. Even though Uriah is relieved of duty, he is uncomfortable with any privilege that would distinguish him from his troop, something that cannot be said of David.

2   S. Bar-Efrat, *Narrative Art in the Bible* (JSOTSup 70; Sheffield: Almond Press, 1989); L. Ryken and T. Longman, *A Complete Literary Guide to the Bible* (Grand Rapids: Zondervan, 1993).

3   In 1 Chronicles 21:1 it is Satan who entices David.

4 First Chronicles 21:6 notes that Joab did not include Levi and Benjamin in the number because the command was abhorrent to him, and 1 Chronicles 27:23–24 notes that Joab did not finish the counting (which may be the same thing as not including Levi and Benjamin).

5 See the same idiom in 1 Samuel 24:5.

6 Here we see, as in 2 Samuel 12, the principle of familial culpability. David's actions stained his entire family. See further J. S. Kaminsky, *Corporate Responsibility in the Hebrew Bible* (JSOTSup 196; Sheffield: Sheffield Academic, 1995).

7 On the capture of Jerusalem from the Jebusites, see ch. 9, "David and Worship."

8 Psalm 111:4 and 145:8 are both focused on praise.

CHAPTER THIRTEEN: DAVID AND MESSIAH

1 The psalm alludes to a great destruction in Jerusalem that is most likely the final demise of the Davidic capital city in 587 B.C.: "broken through all his walls and reduced his strongholds to ruins" (89:40); "all who pass by . . . scorn" (89:41; cf. 1 Kings 9:7–8); "the taunts of all the nations" (89:50).

2 J. B. Pritchard, *Ancient Near Eastern Texts Relating to the Old Testament*. 3rd ed. (Princeton, NJ: Princeton University, 1969), 308.

3 Boda, *Haggai/Zechariah* (Grand Rapids: Zondervan, 2004), 29; cf. E. M. Meyers, "The Shelomith Seal and Aspects of the Judean Restoration: Some Additional Reconsiderations," *EI* 18 (1985): 33–38.

4 See M. J. Boda, "Figuring the Future: The Prophets and the Messiah," in *Messiah*, ed. S. E. Porter (McMaster New Testament Studies; Grand Rapids: Eerdmans, 2007).

5 Psalm 89:52 is not part of the psalm proper, but rather the closing doxology of Book III which stretches from Psalm 73 to 89.

6 Notice how both sections begin with an encounter between prophet and king "at the aqueduct of the Upper Pool, on the road to the Washerman's Field" (7:3; 36:2).

7 Notice how Isaiah 7–12 mentions the names of both of Isaiah's children: Shear-Jashub ("a remnant will return," 7:3) and Maher-Shalal-Hash-Baz ("quick to the plunder," 8:3), but also plays on these names in subsequent prophecies: 10:6 (Maher-Shalal-Hash-Baz) and

10:21–22; cf. 11:11, 16 (Shear-Jashub). Notice also how Isaiah calls not only his sons, but also himself a sign and then plays on his own name in 12:2 ("Yahweh is salvation"). The name Maher-Shalal-Hash-Baz looks to the discipline not only of Israel (Northern Kingdom), but also of Judah (Southern Kingdom) in the period of Hezekiah. But the name Shear-Jashub looks to God's plan through discipline to create a purified remnant for himself. Key to this is the trust in Yahweh for salvation, suggested by the name Isaiah.

8 As I have argued in Boda, "Figuring," as well as in an earlier chapter (ch. 3, "David and Anointing"), three roles were "anointed" or called "Messiah" (anointed one) in ancient Israel, the king, the priest, and the prophet. This helps us to understand why there is such a diversity of "messianic" hope in the period just prior to Jesus; see John 1:19–28; 7:40–44. At Qumran there was an expectation of two messiahs, one priestly and one royal; see Craig A. Evans, "Diarchic Messianism in the Dead Sea Scrolls and the Messianism of Jesus of Nazareth," in *The Dead Sea Scrolls: Fifty Years After Their Discovery, Proceedings of the Jerusalem Congress, July 20–25, 1997*, ed. Lawrence H. Schiffman, Emanuel Tov, and James C. VanderKam (Jerusalem: Israel Exploration Society, 2000), 558–67.

9 The image here is not certain. The term *geza'* (often translated as stump) can refer to tree growth at the end of its life (Job 14:8) or beginning (Isa. 40:24).

10 The reference to the Davidic house in Isaiah 22 should not be viewed as a transference of the Davidic promise to a different line, but rather as a reference to tension between two key officials in the Davidic court in the time of Hezekiah (Eliakim, Shebna) over who had authority to direct the court officials. There is a passing reference to the rule of a righteous king in Isaiah 32:1, but nothing specific can be discerned; see H. G. M. Williamson, *Variations on a Theme: King, Messiah, and Servant in the Book of Isaiah* (Carlisle: Paternoster, 1998), 62–72, who sees this as a proverb on the ideal king, but not referring to a specific future figure. Isaiah 33:17 speaks of seeing the king in his beauty. It is possible that these are references to Yahweh as king as 33:5, 10, 22 suggest.

11 Other important vocabulary associated with the servant in Isaiah 40–66 is "chosen" (42:1; 43:10; 44:1–2; 45:4; 49:7; 65:9, 15) and

the encouragement formula: "Do not fear, for I am with you" (41:10, 13–14; 43:1, 5; 44:2).

12 A point traditionally argued in Jewish interpretation of Isaiah 40–66.

13 A point traditionally argued in Christian interpretation of Isaiah 40–66.

14 It appears that the mention of the priestly figure belongs to a secondary level in the Jeremianic tradition, but is no scribal mistake for it is mentioned three times. Evidence of its secondary character can be discerned in the fact that the Zemah prophecy was clearly limited to the royal house, that the reference to the priestly covenant in verse 21 is obtrusive, and that there is no mention of the priestly figure in 33:23-26.

INDEX OF SCRIPTURE

16:13–14—35
16:14–23—105
16:18—35
17—67, 71
17:4–7—68
17:8–10—68
17:12—68
17:12–15—68
17:16—55, 69
17:17–19—69
17:25, 69
17:26–27, 69
17:33—69
17:37—68–69
17:38—70
17:45—70
17:55–56—70
17:57–58—70
18:1–4—124
18:3—124, 125
18:7—61
18:12—35
18:14—35, 126
18:23—126
18:28—35
18:42—126
19:20—35
20—125, 128
20:8—125
20:14—126, 127, 129
20:14–15—127
20:15—127
20:16—127
20:17—124
20:31—125
20:42—127
21–22—115
21:11—61
22:10—71, 72
23:2—72
23:4—72
23:6—71, 72
23:9–13—72
23:15–18—126, 128

23:16–18—124
23:17—61
24—142, 143
24:1–22—61
24:20—61
26:7–14—61
26:8—61
28:6—71
28:6–7—72
29:5—61
30:7–8—72
30:8—72
31—61, 128

2 Samuel—10, 14, 71, 103, 127

1—61
1:25–27—125
2–4—101
2:1—72
2:1–7—32
3:9–10—61
3:21—124
4—61
4:4—128
5—102
5–10—133
5:1–5—32, 52
5:17–25—71
5:19—72
5:23—72
6:1–11—133
6:5—102
6:16—103
6:17—44
6:20—103
6:21—103
7—4, 41, 43–47, 56, 136, 141, 149, 162
7:1—41
7:1–2—115
7:3—35
7:4—44
7:5—41
7:8–9a—43, 44

7:8–16—54
7:9b–16—43, 44
7:10—26
7:10–11—44, 115
7:10–16—20
7:11–16—32
7:12—25
7:12–13—115
7:13–15—43
7:14—4, 47, 56
7:14a—46
7:14b—46
7:15—46, 48, 140
7:16—43
7:17—44
7:18–19—44
7:20–21—44
7:22—44
7:23–24—44
7:23–26—44
7:25–26—44, 48
8:11—72
8:15—78
9—128, 140
9:1—126, 128
9:3—128–29
9:7—128
11—28, 133, 134
11–12—134
11–20—135
11:1—133
11:27—134
12—134, 135
12:5–6—78, 136
12:7–8—136
12:9—136
12:10–12—136
12:13—136
12:20—33
13—62, 135
13–20—136
13:37–39—62
14—62
14–19—135
14:2—33
14:4–20—78

5:1—160
5:2-5a—160
6:8—126
6:16—160
7:12—80

Nahum
1:3—139

Haggai
1-2—150
1:1—161
1:12-14—161
2:1-4—161
2:20-23—161

Zechariah
1-8—150
3:1-10—161, 162
4:6-10—161, 162
6:9-15—161, 162
7-8—162
9-14—162
9:9-10—162
9:10—80
12:8—162
12:10—162
12:12—162
13:1—162
14:9—162

Malachi
2:1-9—43
2:17—125
4—147

Matthew
1—3
1:1—3, 27
1:6—3
1:17—3
1:20—3
3:13-17—36
3:17—47
5-7—146

5:44—130
6:10—63
6:25-34—84
9:27—3
12:3—3
12:23—3
15:22—3
19:21—84
20:30-31—3
21:9—3
21:15—3
22:42—3
22:43—3
22:45—3
28:18-20—64

Mark
1:9-11—36
2:25—3
10:47-48—3
11:10—3
12:35—3
12:36—3
12:36-37—3

Luke
1:27—3
3:21-22—36
3:22—47
4:18-19—82-83
6:3-5—3
12:22-34—84
18:22—84

John
1:14—95, 119, 143
1:32-34—36, 37
2:19-22—95, 119, 143
4—94, 96
4:20—94
4:21-24—95
4:25-26—95
13:1—129
13:34—130
13:35—130

14-16—37
14:16-17—37
15:12—130
15:13—130
15:17—130

Acts—89
1—63
1:4-5—37
1:16—3
2—36, 83
2:25-32—47
2:29-30—3
2:29-36—64
2:36—64
2:42-47—110
2:44-45—83
2:44-47—90
3:25—27
4—83
4:25—3
4:32-35—90
4:32-37—83
7:45—3
13:22—3
13:33—47
13:33-34—47

Romans
1:3—4
2:4—122
4:16-17—27
6:1—143

1 Corinthians
3:16—120
6:19—98, 120
10:1-13—145
11:17-34—84
14:26—109

2 Corinthians
3:7-18—120
6:18—4

Dr. Mark Boda spent his early life in the Academy setting, growing up in the home of a seminary professor and president in Western Canada. He ministered in pastorates in both Toronto and Philadelphia and served in campus ministry in Toronto before joining the faculty of Canadian Bible College and Theological Seminary in Regina, Saskatchewan, where he served from 1994 until 2003. Presently he is professor in the Faculty of Theology at McMaster University and holds the Chair in Old Testament at McMaster Divinity College in Hamilton, Ontario where he enjoys teaching and mentoring students.

Mark began his education at Alliance University College (then Canadian Bible College) where he received a Bachelor of Theology in 1984. After his first pastorate he studied for the Master of Divinity at Westminster Theological Seminary (1991) before receiving his Ph.D. at the University of Cambridge (1996).

Dr. Boda has published over forty-five articles on the Old Testament and Semitic Languages in scholarly journals, collected essays, and dictionaries. He is author of four books and editor of seven others on various issues related to the Old Testament and Christian Theology.

Mark and his wife, Beth, gladly and passionately mentor their three boys (David, Stephen, and Matthew) in the life of the Spirit.